VICTOR
OVER
VICTIM

The Bruce Walsh Story

VICTOR
OVER
VICTIM

The Bruce Walsh Story

As told to Sybrand Mostert

Human & Rousseau
Cape Town   Pretoria   Johannesburg

First Published in 2003 by Human & Rousseau
40 Heerengracht, Cape Town

10 9 8 7 6 5 4 3 2 1

Publisher: Marianne Nicol
Editor: Sybrand Mostert
Design and Typesetting: Etienne van Duyker,
Alinea Studio, Cape Town
Cover photograph: Kelly Walsh
Printing and binding: Paarl Print,
Oosterland Street, Paarl

ISBN 0 7981 4382 7

THANKS

Robyn Wheeler – for refusing to write this for me, instead encouraging me to do it myself.

Dee Byrne-Daily – for advice and encouragement in the early stages of this project.

Carl Eichstadt – for his input regarding "leadership" and for believing in me and giving me work shortly after I became unemployed.

Marianne Nicol – for the role she played in making this project a reality.

Sybrand Mostert – for his penmanship, his good humour and his sensitivity.

Magda Herbst – for her transcripts of the sometimes not very clear tapes.

Carolyn, Garth and Ronald – for their input and for their willingness to revisit their emotions associated with that time.

Linda Kantor – for input, handled as sensitively as ever regarding my sessions with her and around "post traumatic stress".

The doctors and medical personnel – for saving my life, for nursing and caring for me with such love and dedication.

Tilly Welsh – for looking after me so well when I came home from hospital.

Standard Bank – for the care, consideration and support given to me and the other staff members involved in the bomb blast.

To God all the glory.

DEDICATION

Between 1995 and 2000 there were a number of bomb blasts in Cape Town. Restaurants, clubs, coffee shops and police stations were targeted.

I would like to dedicate this book to all of those who were killed or injured in these incidents.

A list of the injured would be too long to give here, but I would like to mention especially the following: my former colleagues, Fanie Schoeman and Brian Duddy, who died after the Planet Hollywood bombing. Nolusindiso Mlolo, a street vendor, who died in the blast outside the Bellville police offices; and those who lost limbs in the bombings: Matty Duddy, Laura Giddinghs (Planet Hollywood), Olivia Milner (St Elmo's), and policewoman Natasha Pillay.

PREFACE

It was not a conscious decision of write this book. Neither was it a deliberate decision to get onto the so-called "motivational" speaking circuit. Both happened quite by accident and almost by default.

The sharing of my experience with others – in an attempt to illustrate the point that while we often have no control of the circumstances we find ourselves in, we can control our response and reaction to those circumstances – happened shortly after I returned to work. The bank where I worked was undergoing some major restructuring, and the staff, especially those in the branches, were extremely rattled and resistant to the changes that were being thrown at them at an alarming rate.

There was nothing else they could do about these changes, other than to resist them or to embrace them.

I used my experience to illustrate that fighting the inevitable is stressful and emotionally draining and that you remain at the mercy of the situation, without any control. I also illustrated that in order to overcome this they needed to "take charge" and to manage their response to what was happening around them.

I started talking to bank staff and soon, by word of mouth, people outside the bank began to hear about my "inspirational" message. They too, began to ask me to speak to them.

So it was that I began to speak to church groups, schools, and women's organisations and later at company conferences, to work teams and to organisations about to embark on major structural changes.

These talks have afforded me the opportunity to travel all over South Africa, neighbouring countries and as far afield as the United States and New Zealand.

Although I was able to stand in front of an audience and share my gruelling experience with them and then relate it to a model of Emotional Intelligence, I was not fully able to come to terms with the senselessness of it all.

It was then that I decided to document the experience in a rational, orderly manner in the hope that this would be my catharsis. Before actually capturing my experience on paper I reflected for many a month on my life to date.

As I thought about certain incidents that had occurred in my life and generally the way my life had unfolded, I came to the conclusion that everything that had happened to me and had moulded me, seemed almost like a preparation that enabled me to cope with the magnitude of the bomb incident.

With this premise in mind I then set about capturing aspects of my life, from childhood to the present. I was able to conceptualise the bomb experience and to take stock of where I am currently, where I am going to and to prioritise those things in my life that are important to me.

The writing turned out to be exactly what I had intended it to be – a cathartic experience.

While working on this project I told people what I was doing and I let a few read what I had written. Invariably they suggested that I publish it in book form. Contact was made with Marianne Nicol at Human & Rousseau Publishers, and she read what I had written as well as a synopsis of what I intended to write and decided that my book needed to be published.

I would request, dear reader, that as you read this book you reflect constantly on your own life journey.

Do you find yourself being trapped in circumstances where external issues seem to control and manage you, or are you the sort of person who is temporarily set back by circumstances but quickly recovers, begins to take charge of the situation and moves on triumphantly?

My wish is that this book should give you food for thought.

PROLOGUE

One day reality intruded upon my world. It was towards the end of September, about a month after the blast.

The sun was rising and as I looked out of the hospital window, I wondered where I was.

I thought to myself: "This is not where I should be. This isn't my bed." I did not recognise the view and I didn't recognise the bed. My first impression was that it must have been one hell of a party that I had been to the night before, because this was not where I was supposed to be.

Strange what tricks one's mind can play.

I thought to myself that it was time for me to get up; find my clothes; find my car and get home.

I was blissfully unaware that I was connected to a battery of machinery behind me, but I knew that I needed to get up.

I struggled to get out of bed, but if you do not have legs you do not get very far. I crashed onto the hospital floor.

The poor ward sister came rushing in.

"Please, Bruce," she said. "You have enough cuts and bruises. You don't have to go and cut your head open." I remember saying to her very vividly, very clearly, through this hole in my throat: "Where am I? What's happened?"

And it was the weirdest, weirdest feeling to be told that Fanie Schoeman, who had been a colleague for so long and with whom I had worked so closely over the last few months, was dead and buried. And Brian Duddy, dead and gone as well.

And then she told me what the bomb had done to me.

She did so very gently, very clearly and with great empathy.

When she had finished I asked to be left alone. I lay there thinking: This can't be true. This can't have happened to me. It is all a bad dream.

Eventually I found the courage to lift the sheets. I looked down. That was reality. Where my legs should have been, there was nothing – just a white sheet. My first reaction was to cry, to cry deeply. Raw animal noises came from my mouth.

As the pain of realisation subsided, I realised that I could not lie there, crying for the rest of my life. That I would have to do something.

And I remember thinking: "These 'bliksems'! They can take my legs and they can take my colleagues. No amount of crying, anger or despair will ever bring them back. But what I will *not* do is give the planters of this bomb the satisfaction that they had taken a full life from me.

I was going to fight to get that back.

CHAPTER I

THE BOMB

I am not a morning person. What is best for me I think, is a nice warm, safe and secure place, so I have always battled to get out of bed in the morning.

That fateful Tuesday morning in the winter of August 1998 was no different.

Invariably I'm awake before the alarm goes off just before 5am – but that doesn't mean that I leap out of bed. I lie there with my eyes closed and rest, waiting for the alarm, enjoying the last warmth and comfort.

This is when the first ritual of my day begins. I think of all the reasons why I should stay in bed longer, for at least another half an hour, or even better, I think of how I could spend the entire day in bed. I go through the whole debate literally every weekday morning.

Then I shrug it off, get out of bed and hit the road for my morning run. I was a keen runner.

On that Tuesday morning I had good enough reason to want to stay at home. It was a winter's morning in Cape Town, cold and dark. I was feeling a bit fluey. I could have justified just letting it all go, but I willed myself up and let my dogs in. They greeted me like a long-lost friend, I fed them and made myself some coffee.

My second ritual of the day is to put on my running gear and go out for a five or six kilometre run, depending on how much time I have available.

That morning as I sat putting on my running shoes, I had no way of knowing that it would be the last time I would put a pair of running shoes on my own two feet. I often wonder what my life would have been like if I had followed my heart that day and stayed in bed.

Be that as it may, soon I was out in the cold, running. I used this time to think through the issues of the day and that Tuesday morning I had major issues to think through.

Safia Lagardien, my second in command, and an industrial psychologist by training, had resigned to join another company in Cape Town. And an equally valuable, but more junior and younger colleague, Claire Thorndyke, had decided to resign at the end of August to emigrate to London with her husband who is an accountant. At the time there was a moratorium on recruitment so I had to juggle their duties and responsibilities among my existing team.

These were the problems I was thinking about when I went for my run, and the dinner that night at Planet Hollywood Restaurant was to say good-bye to Safia and Claire.

After the run I prepared for work, put my dogs out, locked up my house and was on the N1 heading for Cape Town and my office by about 6:40am.

My office at Standard Bank was in Adderley Street on the Foreshore. Traffic at that time of the morning is already quite horrendous, but I found that leaving home between 6:30 and 6:40 allowed me enough time to get to work before 7:30.

I enjoyed that half an hour before the business day officially begins. It gave me time to access my e-mail, check my in-baskets, prepare my diary, and to get all my ducks in a row for the day ahead.

That Tuesday morning, Carl Eichstadt, a colleague from Group Human Resources in Johannesburg had made an appointment with me to discuss certain issues and aspects of a development program that he wanted to initiate in the Western Cape.

I had my meeting with Carl and we spoke at length about the program that he was to put in place, and in which I would be a key player.

Later I met Carl for lunch in a street café in Adderley Street. At the time I was busy completing a Master's Degree and I discussed with him the possibility of getting international experience in the UK or America. We spoke about our future in Standard

Bank and as we got to the end of lunch I invited Carl to join us for our evening meal at Planet Hollywood.

He declined, and at the office, the afternoon flew by all too quickly. At the end of the day, at about 5 o'clock, I hit the traffic home. There I sorted my dogs out and took them for a little run along the park next to my house.

Just before leaving for Planet Hollywood, I received two phone calls. One was from my friend Ronald, a medical doctor in George who had phoned to chat and to find out how the day had been. I can remember mentioning to him that I was feeling a bit fluey and I really didn't feel like the dinner that awaited me. He suggested that I cancel and have an early night.

I told him I couldn't do that. I had to say good-bye to Claire Thorndyke and Safia Lagardien.

Then Manfred, another friend who lives in Plattekloof, just around the corner, called. From the patio of his home you have a breathtaking view of the city of Cape Town and Table Mountain. He said it was such a lovely evening and he was having friends around – wouldn't I like to come and join them for drinks and dinner.

I said I already had an arrangement at Planet Hollywood, but he none the less invited me for a glass of wine on my way to Planet Hollywood. And again I declined, because it would make me late and I didn't think it was appropriate for me be late.

I left home, leaving my bedside radio playing and strategic lights burning as a security measure.

A creature of habit, I parked my car in my usual parking place at the V&A Waterfront, beneath the Woolworths shopping complex. I took a slow stroll through the shopping centre, little knowning what awaited me. I had not the faintest idea that in a matter of a few minutes my entire life would change forever.

I can remember walking through that shopping complex, window-shopping, totally unconcerned, and looking forward to the meal that lay ahead. Looking forward to spending some quality time with my colleagues.

I walked down towards the restaurant complex and arrived just before 7 o'clock. I stood at the entrance looking in. It was dark with neon lights flashing and all sorts of symbols of the rock era hung all over the place, guitars and so on. Dark and loud, the music quite overwhelming.

At the time it seemed a warm, inviting and successful restaurant.

I told the maître de' I was there to join the Standard Bank party. Some of our group had already arrived, and we were asked to wait in the bar area until everyone was there.

As I came in, I saw Matty, Brian, Fanie, Antoinette, Gay and her partner at a table near the bar. I joined them.

Our table was about four metres from the bar, which was made of solid wood, and had a foot rest. Drinks and glasses lined the back panel.

Fanie Schoeman, who had just turned 50, was a Human Resources Manager in my department, and a valuable member of my team. He had worked at Standard Bank for many years, slowly making his way up the ladder. He was a good, steady, salt-of-the-earth type of guy. He knew everyone, and everyone knew him.

He had been battling prostate cancer, and had just been given the news that the cancer was in remission. He had a clean bill of health.

That night Fanie and Antoinette were feeling pretty buoyant, quite jubilant and in a celebratory mood.

Fanie had also applied for the post I now held, but despite my getting the job he was a loyal and supportive member of my team. We worked well together, the two of us. I had only met Antoinette once prior to this meeting and so I was looking forward to having a chat and getting to know her a little better.

Fanie and Antoinette were in their second marriage, and both had adult kids from their first marriages. Antoinette was always busy at home, running their B&B cottages.

Brian and Matty Duddy were also at the table. Matty was our departmental secretary and she certainly looked after me. Her husband Brian worked in our home loans division.

They were a couple in their 50s with two adult children, but Matty and Brian really loved each other. They were still like new young lovers. They drove to work together, and spent their lunch times together. They meant everything to each other. Often, Matty told me, they would stop on their way home to Fish Hoek and watch the whales at play in the bay.

They were soul mates, and never a day went by that they didn't speak at least two or three times to each other on the phone. Matty told me they lived for each other, their children and their family.

(A corner in the pub at Standard Bank is now called Duddy's Corner. It is dedicated to this couple, who were always there, together, on a Friday night.)

Gay Tyler, a personnel officer was also with us. Gay was single and she had brought along a new partner, Johan Dippenaar, that evening, to whom she introduced all of us. Gay was a shy, reserved and private person, whom I did not know that well. As I got to the table after greeting everybody, I was introduced to Gay's partner.

The restaurant was cavernous, dark, with flashing neon lights all over the place. Slowly our eyes adjusted to the dark. Music blared.

The bar was on our left, on an elevated platform. The dining room, which could probably seat about 150 people, was on the right.

I cannot recall how many people were in the restaurant, but it was still early, and I think there was only a handful of people at the bar, and at some tables nearby. Some were strolling around, admiring the rock memorabilia, and some were seated farther away from the pub.

We were all at the table closest to the pub. Another young girl, Laura Giddings, who was there on holiday with her family, from Britain, also lost her leg in the blast. They must have been sitting very close to us.

"As the boss I'll buy the first round," I told everyone. "But after that – it's everyone for themselves."

I took the drinks order and Fanie and Brian joined me as I strolled over to the bar to place the order. By now it was just after 7pm.

Another colleague, Claire Thorndyke and her husband, Andrew Parris arrived, and after greeting us walked towards our table.

Claire and Andrew had just recently got married. Claire was a senior personnel officer with the bank – highly competent and had the world at her feet. Andrew was an accountant, and the two of them were going to seek their fortune overseas.

Fanie, Brian and I got to the bar, and leaned on it, trying to chat over the loud music. I remember that I placed the order, and then the barman moved away to mix our drinks. I was in the centre, between Fanie and Brian.

The last thing I remember is placing my wallet on the counter.

Then my world exploded. The bomb blast hit us with an awesome force. I remember a flash of intense pain – and then nothing. I felt out of my body, floating in mid-air. I remember seeing dust, debris. There was blood all over me.

Fanie, Brian and I took the brunt of the blast. The bomb had apparently been taped to the inside of the bar's footrest. The footrest was a solid wood piece, running along the entire pub.

The three of us were standing at the epicentre, virtually over the lethal device.

I must have been flung high into the air by the blast, as police later found pieces of my shirt in the shattered rafters.

I landed on the floor. I felt helpless. No pain.

I remember there was chaos all around me. I saw this as from a dream world. Everything was happening very slowly. Screaming, shouting, noise. I could not move, feel anything, or do anything.

Andrew was lying next to me on the floor. He was conscious throughout the ordeal, and saw what the bomb had done to Brian, Fanie and myself.

He was in extreme pain. Next to him lay his young wife Claire. She was also still conscious. (In fact she was able to direct the paramedics when help arrived to the worst injured and to tell them who they were.)

Andrew was crying and telling Claire that he could not feel his legs. He was afraid that he too, had had his feet blown off. He was badly injured, and Claire just did not want him to see his legs.

She kept saying to him: "You are going to be all right, just lie still."

She kept reassuring him that his legs were not blown off. When Andrew was later loaded into an ambulance he was able to lift his head and look at his feet. He saw that his shoes were still there.

They were where the feet should be. This gave him a sense of great relief.

I lay there, I don't remember for how long. But I do remember somebody shouting: "He's choking! He can't breathe, help him!" I felt hands touching me and my body being covered. Suddenly I was cold, I was shivering. Somebody turned my head to the side, and that is when I lost consciousness.

Fanie, Brian and myself were the most seriously injured. We all lost our feet. As we had been virtually standing over the bomb, we were all badly burnt and had massive injuries, plus internal bleeding.

It was a miracle that I survived.

Fanie died that night. Brian was knocked unconscious in the blast, and never regained consciousness. He died five days later.

When the blast went off Claire and Andrew were walking towards the table, with Andrew just behind Claire. Andrew partially shielded Claire. His calf muscles were ripped off, and he also bore the full brunt of the blast. Claire was badly burnt, and had foot injuries. Her ear drums were badly affected.

Of those of us who were at the table, Matty was badly burnt and both her legs were severely damaged. One leg had to be amputated, and she struggled for a long time to regain some use in her other leg.

Antoinette's face and arms were burnt and she hurt her leg. She lost her husband, and still suffers leg problems. Gay is slightly hearing impaired and has a scarred face from the blast. I think that her partner, whom she had brought along for us to meet that night, was only slightly injured.

While this was happening, the remainder of our colleagues were still arriving. Some were parking their cars, some were walking towards the restaurant, and some were still driving from their homes along the highways and byways towards the Waterfront.

Carolyn Stewart, the occupational health nurse at the Standard Bank, was parking her car when she heard the blast. "Please, God, don't let it be Planet Hollywood!" she said to herself, realising it could have possibly been a bomb.

Carolyn is Irish and from the North of Ireland, from the Belfast area. She had arrived in South Africa as a young girl. So she is familiar with bomb blasts and terror attacks. As she ran towards the Planet Hollywood, amongst the chaos and the mayhem people were running and shouting: "There's a bomb! There's been an explosion!" Ambulance sirens wailed and a sense of fear filled the air.

"I was employed as the Occupational Health Practitioner at Standard Bank, Cape Town from 1992–2001 and formed part of the of the Human Resources team," says Carolyn.

"In August 1998 the H.R. team (under the leadership of Bruce Walsh) organised a 'leaving do' for two of our colleagues at Planet Hollywood. We had arranged to meet at 7pm for drinks and to have dinner at 7.30pm. As I had a sore back on that day I decided to arrive just before dinner started at 7.30pm.

"When I arrived at the Waterfront I could hear the sirens of fire engines and other rescue vehicles. I walked towards Planet Hollywood and saw that it had been cordoned off with red and white tape to the rear of the building.

"My first thought was that there had been a bomb, but I tried to rationalise by thinking it was a fire in the kitchen. I then met several colleagues who told me that a bomb had gone off. We were all horrified and could see a colleague who had been inside when the bomb went off. She was sitting outside. She had injuries to her leg and told us that Bruce and six other colleagues had all been inside. They were all injured. We didn't know the extent of their injuries.

"The ambulance crew were already on the scene. We were advised to move away from the scene for our own safety as they suspected that there could be another device inside.

"I went to a friend's house and phoned around the various hospitals to find out where our injured colleagues had been taken. After many phone calls I managed to find out where most of them were. A friend, Chris, accompanied me, firstly to Somerset Hospital as we suspected Bruce and another colleague had been taken there.

"I had been describing Bruce to the sister on the phone by the colour of his hair, height, etc. But these descriptions were of no use at the time – as I was to see later. We met two more colleagues at the hospital who had recognised Bruce's clothes, his shoes and BMW key ring and said he was in theatre.

"I asked the sister if I could see Bruce when he came out of theatre. She then led me down the corridor and into a room. I was thinking that I was going to see Bruce but instead she showed me the dead body of another colleague. This was a great shock to me and a sight I wish I had never seen.

"Eventually I was able to see Bruce in the intensive care unit. I had spoken to the surgeon earlier on. He had explained the extent of Bruce's injuries and the fact that both legs had been amputated as well as having 40% of his body burned. When I saw Bruce he was unrecognisable. His hair was all burnt away and his face was very swollen. Once again this was a great shock.

"By this time it was nearly midnight and we decided to try get in touch with Bruce's brother in Natal as well a close friend in George. With help from colleagues and friends we managed to accomplish this.

"Chris and I then went to Groote Schuur Hospital to see another colleague who had inhalation burns, hearing loss and shrapnel wounds.

"By 3am I had returned home, exhausted and shocked but surviving on adrenalin. By 8am the following morning I was at the airport to meet a friend of Bruce's. We then went to the hospital to see Bruce.

"I remember the sister who was looking after Bruce saying: "If I were him I wouldn't want to live." I remember thinking: "But you don't know Bruce. He is a fighter and he won't give up easily."

That morning I attended a debriefing session for our colleagues at the bank following the bomb blast. It helped to listen to how other people were feeling and to normalise our own feelings. Later that day I visited another two injured colleagues at Cape Town Medi Clinic and chatted to the matron about their condition. Sadly one of them was severely injured and later died. The other had lost a leg below the knee."

Carolyn was a pillar of strength amongst the chaos outside Planet Hollywood.

She coordinated what was happening, she kept a record of who went with whom to which hospital. She made a point of contacting next of kin and family members, of informing the General Manager, Ernst Ward-Cox, of the bomb blast that evening, and throughout the night she diligently tracked down people, relatives, family. She didn't sleep throughout that night.

It was Carolyn who got hold of Italia Bonnenelli who was my direct boss. Italia was the head of Human Resources at Standard Bank's retail banking operations. Carolyn called Italia and told her that Fanie, myself, Matty and Brian had been injured in a bomb blast.

It was Carolyn who got hold of Fanie and Antoinette's family. It was Carolyn who got hold of Matty and Brian's children.

Then it struck Carolyn that she knew almost nothing about my family.

I had only arrived in Cape Town from Johannesburg a year before. I didn't know too many people in Cape Town and I was a very private person. Two of the most important things to me were my privacy and my independence.

And Carolyn was struck by the fact that there was nobody that she could contact to inform about me. Then she remembered that I had mentioned I had a friend who is an oncologist in George.

Through sheer accident, Carolyn too had a friend who is an oncologist, but in Cape Town. Amidst the chaos and confusion of that evening Carolyn called her friend who happened to know my friend in George, Ronald Uijs.

But no-one could reach Ronald as his cell phone was switched off, and eventually a friend of his, who had been alerted by a radiographer who worked with Ronald, scaled his garden wall at 2am to give him the news.

While this was happening Carolyn and Italia were trying to get hold of my brother Garth in Durban.

CHAPTER II

HOSPITAL

Garth takes up the story.

On the Tuesday night, the 25th of August 1998, as I reached to turn off the 8 o'clock news, subtitles reading "Bomb Blast – Planet Holleywood" flashed on the screen.

As I climbed into bed I remarked to my wife Shelley that the cowardly criminal element of our society were trying to shatter the morale of our Rainbow Nation.

It was unclear to me at that stage that it was a group possibly aligned to other terror attacks against American targets across Africa that was responsible. I also had no idea that my brother Bruce had been in the restaurant when the bomb went off.

At 6.45am the next day I phoned a builder currently doing minor alterations around our property to remind him of a few tasks he should complete. I had barely put the phone down when it rang.

Thinking that it was the builder calling back I was totally unprepared for the caller's message.

"Your brother Bruce has been badly injured in the Planet Hollywood bomb blast and his chances of survival are slim. I suggest you get to Cape Town as quickly as possible." It had taken Bruce's colleagues nearly 12 hours to track down his next of kin!

Filled with unexpected emotion and some dread, I phoned my sister Dorothy, who became as distraught as I was. We decided to get the next available flight to Cape Town.

We arrived in Cape Town later that afternoon and were met by Standard Bank officials who took us to the hospital.

As children Bruce and I were close, as our mother never let us do anything separately. We always had to go everywhere together. We even wore the same clothing.

In our teens I rebelled against this and many other things. I became a typical Durban surfer, a *joller*, experimenting with soft drugs and booze, hitting the waves whenever I could.

Bruce was a "goody two shoes", which irritated and embarrassed me, especially when my buddies came to visit. I was this nerd's younger brother.

As we moved into adulthood, we kind of grew

apart. We kept in touch and we visited each other from time to time, but that was about it. I was in Durban, and Bruce in Johannesburg. A bond that kept us in touch was my daughter, with whom Bruce developed a close relationship.

But that was all to change in the following days.

While Dorothy and I were travelling to Cape Town, family members in Natal had also alerted a cousin in Cape Town, Kelly Walsh, to meet us at the hospital.

When we arrived there I was quietly ushered into the Intensive Care ward where Bruce was. I couldn't believe my eyes – that this person in the bed was my brother.

I was stunned by this body, criss-crossed with pipes protruding from his nose and mouth, the body swollen beyond recognition and badly burnt.

Shocked, I turned to the nurse next to me and asked: "But where's Bruce?" That is him, she said.

I was shattered, my legs reduced to jelly. Bruce was beyond recognition. A charred, swollen mass. And so began a journey of roller-coasting emotions.

For a few days it was touch and go whether Bruce would make it – whether he would live through this.

These were Bruce's injuries:

- What was left of both his legs had to be amputated below the knee.
- All the bones in his left arm had disintegrated in the blast, and the arm, which was badly

deformed, was bleeding profusely. The nerves controlling the left hand had been severed, which meant that he could not use his hand at all.

- Bruce had second-degree burns over 40% of his entire body. (Third-degree burns are the worst you can sustain.) When you are burnt your body retains water. His head was the size of a watermelon, and all the hair on his head had been singed, including eyebrows and eyelashes.
- Debris from the bomb had infiltrated his lungs and he had to have a tracheotomy to help him breathe. A tracheotomy is a device inserted through a hole cut in the throat to reach the lungs.
- Shrapnel: eight surgeons had to work on Bruce when he was first admitted to remove pieces of the bomb from his wounds. He still has scars today.
- His skull was fractured, and as a result, there was bleeding on the brain.
- His eardrums had burst, and doctors feared that he would be deaf.
- He had lost so much blood that he was given 46 units in the first 24 hours after the blast.
- Doctors also feared that the impact of the blast on his skull could have caused brain damage.
- The biggest concern was the internal bleeding that could not be contained, and the fact that his internal organs were slowly shutting down.

Ronald, a close family friend and himself a medical specialist, had arranged accommodation for my sister and I at a colleague's home.

Our trip to Cape Town became a ritual of daily trips to the hospital interacting with Kelly, Ronald, Bruce's numerous colleagues, friends, doctors and the concerned public and press.

We prayed, we cried and we celebrated any slight improvement we thought Bruce had made. However we were disturbed by the news that Bruce might be brain damaged, that his hearing would be reduced to about 10% and that he still risked the amputation of his left arm, all this after he had already lost his legs.

Our group of Kelly, Ronald, Dorothy and myself became a tight-knit one planning and discussing Bruce's way forward should he survive.

It was however a tense period tip-toeing around each other's emotions.

At this time a good friend of Bruce's, Thomas O' Reilley, who had taught with him in Durban but had subsequently moved to Cape Town, arranged for the last rites to be performed for Bruce.

Bruce is godfather to Thomas's youngest son, Edward. Thomas is a devout Catholic and when the news was out that Bruce was critical and it was unlikely that he would make it, Thomas decided that Bruce, even as a lapsed Catholic at that stage, should receive the last rites.

So he arranged with a priest friend to perform the ceremony. This apparently was carried out only after the two of them had built up enough Dutch courage at a nearby pub to do so.

Not satisfied with the job done by this man, Thomas, just to be sure and as only an Irishman would, arranged for a second bout of the last rites to be performed on Bruce. (In a much more sober atmosphere this time.)

After 15 days our group – Kelly, Dorothy, Ronald and myself met with the chief physician.

Besides Bruce's horrific injuries, the biggest problem was that the doctors could not stop the internal bleeding, and as a result his internal organs were shutting down.

His body wasn't responding to the medication they were giving him to stop the internal bleeding – and that, they thought, was going to kill him.

Bruce was still unconscious.

During this time, I must say, the doctors, despite all the problems, always remained cautiously optimistic. They kept us informed of all the possibilities, though.

They would say things like "He will possibly have only 10 % hearing," and "he could possibly as a result of the impact of the blast to his head and the subsequent fractured skull, be brain damaged," or "We might have to remove the left arm".

They suggested that maybe Bruce should be

removed from the life-support systems and nature should be allowed to take its course. But at no stage did they ever say he was going to die.

In fact they always said: "Where there is life, there is hope". In the meeting with the chief physician I suggested that as Bruce had shown very little, if any improvement, after two weeks that the life-support systems should be switched off.

I was worn down by the days of emotion at his bedside, and worrying what sort of life my brother would have without legs, an arm, and probably deaf.

We also did not know whether he was brain damaged.

How would he live? It was a hellish decision to have to make. Our sister Dorothy, however, was horrified by this suggestion. (I cannot remember Ronald's thinking at the time but probably with his extensive medical background he might have shared the sentiment.)

But the chief physician said that there was still hope, and that we should persevere.

Two days later, a long 17 days after the bomb blast, the internal bleeding eventually stopped and Bruce regained consciousness.

While Bruce was still unconscious and struggling for life, Dorothy, Kelly, Ronald and I would go to a pub in nearby Green Point and celebrate whenever there was any slight improvement.

When he regained consciousness we shared a bottle of French champagne.

Seeing the state that Bruce was in after the bomb brought back that closeness we had shared as children.

I was outraged by the deed. I was angry. Anger is perhaps too mild a word to describe the rage I felt for the people who had done this. I wanted to hurt them with all the power I could produce.

I am not sure that I have forgiven what they did to my brother.

But at the same time I am extremely proud of how he has dealt with it.

We are closer now then ever, and chat on the phone weekly.

Being confronted with Bruce's possible death was extremely traumatic and often I would weep when he was at death's door. I never showed that degree of grief in front of the others, because I felt I needed to be strong.

But in quiet moments I felt the anguish of potentially losing a brother whom I love.

CHAPTER III

INVESTIGATION

In November 1998 when I was at home recovering, there was a flash on the main evening news that the police investigating the Planet Hollywood bombing had discovered a piece of a sleeve – actually the cuff – from a shirt in the roof of the restaurant.

The news item said that police were convinced that the blue and white checked shirt had belonged to the bomber, and the identification of the shirt could lead them to the man.

A sample of the shirt was displayed by the investigating officer on the news. He held up an exact replica of the make and size of the shirt.

The officer said that the shirt was special, and

only a few hundred had been sold at certain selected boutiques in South Africa.

The police had identified where the shirts had been sold in Cape Town, and "had certain leads" because of this.

A prime suspect, the policeman said, was a German who had bought one of the shirts in Cape Town.

I was astonished, gobsmacked, I could say. This shirt, which was leading to the "breakthrough", was mine!

Next day I called the policeman, and told him that "the shirt" was actually mine.

There was silence at the other end of the line.

"But how could it be yours? It is impossible – we found it in the ceiling," the policeman replied.

I told him that I was at the centre of the blast and had been hurled into the air. My left arm had been badly hurt in the blast.

Soon an entourage of policemen was at my home with samples of the shirt. I identified the shirt as the one I had been wearing, and also gave them the receipt I had kept when I bought the shirt.

When they saw the state that my arm was in, the policemen sheepishly left.

That angle of the investigation died a quiet death.

Since I was so badly injured by the bomb no government or police official has ever informed me about the progress of the investigation, or who the suspects in the case are.

When Matty Duddy and I were in hospital and

recuperating at home, there was also total silence from officialdom.

No-one has ever been arrested in connection with the Planet Hollywood bombing. As far as I know, the case is still open.

When I was writing this book I requested an interview, and an update from the police on the investigation. I was told to go through the formal channels of submitting a request to the local Commissioner.

Questions about the case that I had sent to the Scorpions, who took over the case from local police, have remained unanswered at the time of going to press.

So with official silence, I have done some research myself. The following pieces of information I found on the Internet.

Firstly to give you some idea of the context in which the bombing took place, here is a time line of events that took place in Cape Town at that time:

1995
December
- People against Gangsterism and Drugs (Pagad) is established.

    The dormitory suburbs of Cape Town on the Cape Flats are largely populated by coloured people, originally the progeny of white settlers, San people, and slaves.

Due to South Africa's earlier race-based political system, coloured people have always lived a twilight existence on the edge of society.

The Cape Flats suburbs are working class, and very poor, with a high unemployment rate. Gangs flourish in these circumstances, and largely rule the local populations.

They probably make up the biggest employers in these areas and generate millions of Rand through drug dealing, extortion and prostitution.

At the same time, there is a strong Muslim community in Cape Town, which holds strong adherence to the dictates of the Koran.

Gang activities in the 1990s were – and still are – a complete anathema to this community.

1996

January – June
■ Pagad holds public meetings, demonstrations and marches.

August
■ Rashaad Staggie (twin brother of Rashied Staggie and co-leader of the Hard Livings, one of the most powerful gangs in the Western Cape) is attacked and killed following a Pagad protest march to his house in London Road, Salt River.
■ Pagad issues an ultimatum to gangs to stop drug dealing. Gangsters respond by threatening to burn down mosques and disrupt schools and

Muslim businesses. They warn Pagad of the dangers of starting a full-scale war.

- Signs of internal division in Pagad begin to emerge with allegations that it has fallen under the control of a radical Islamic group, Qibla. Qibla leader, Achmat Cassiem, is profiled in the media as a "holy warrior".

1997

- Increasing violence on the Cape Flats is attributed to inter-gang conflict, as well as attacks and counter-attacks involving both the gangs and Pagad.
- Many religious leaders move to distance themselves from Pagad.
- Community radio station 786 is found guilty of biased reporting and accused of inciting people to violence. An article in a British newspaper alleges that the Islamic Unity Convention (IUC) is behind the formation of Radio 786 and is using it to promote Qibla's radical political agenda.

April

- A drug dealer's home in the Bo-Kaap is attacked and burnt down.

September

- Several mosques and well-known Muslim businessmen are attacked and a number of people are killed. Press reports link the attacks to the continuing "war" between Pagad and the gangs.

November
- National Coordinator Aslam Toefy resigns from Pagad. There are suggestions that he disagrees with Qibla leaders about strategy and the use of violence.

1998
- A string of prominent gang members are killed in drive-by shootings in the first quarter of 1998.

January
- Lansdowne police station is bombed

May
- Pipe bombs are thrown at the homes of two wealthy Muslim businessmen.

June
- Media reports of a new Pagad "hit squad" appear. The group is said to be independent of the group's existing military wing (known as the G-force).
- Mowbray police station is damaged in a bomb attack.

July
- The home of prominent academic, Ebrahim Moosa, is the target of a pipe bomb attack.

August
- An explosion outside the Bellville offices of the special police task team investigating Pagad results in the death of a street vendor.
- Planet Hollywood Restaurant is bombed, leaving two people dead and 26 injured. The attack is said to be a response to recent attacks by the United States of America on alleged terrorist bases in Sudan and Afghanistan.
- Pagad restates its commitment to fighting gangsterism and drugs. They also criticise the media for holding Pagad responsible for bomb attacks.

November
- Ismail April (alias Bobby Mongrel), leader of The Mongrels gang, and Americans gang supremo, Jackie Lonte, are gunned down.
- Four attempted murder charges against Pagad's National Coordinator, Abdus Salaam Ebrahim, are withdrawn because evidence has been tampered with. Attempted murder cases against Ebrahim and nine other Pagad members are postponed when two witnesses are shot.

December
- A bomb explodes outside a synagogue in Wynberg.
- There are bomb attacks in Retreat, Lansdowne and Sherwood Park over the Christmas and New Year holidays.

1999

January

- The New Year is ushered in with a car bomb explosion at the V & A Waterfront. Days later an attack on the Claremont police station is said to be the work of vigilantes.
- Bombs explode outside the Caledon Square and Woodstock police stations.
- Legislation designed to curb urban terrorism is introduced in Parliament.
- Senior detective, Bennie Lategan, is "assassinated" on the Cape Flats. He had been investigating the New Year's Day car bombing, as well as the alleged role in the violence of prominent members of both Pagad and the gangs.

March

- Muslim businessman Rafiek Parker is killed in a drive-by shooting in Athlone. A similar incident at Cape Town International Airport results in the death of a senior detective working on urban terror cases.

April

- Reports of a "hit list" of prominent Muslim businessmen coincide with the shooting of Gatesville businessman, Adam Vinoos. Later in the year a Pagad member named Ragmoedien Jeneker is charged with the murder of Vinoos.

- Pagad is alleged to have an extortion racket demanding protection money from Muslim businessmen.
- Well-known gangster Glen Kahn is killed in a drive-by shooting.

May
- The US State Department classifies Pagad and Qibla as terrorist groups.
- A car bomb explodes outside Athlone police station.

August
- The new elite police unit, the Scorpions, takes over the investigation of urban terror and organised crime.

November
- The Blah Bar in Green Point is bombed. Homophobia is thought to be a possible motive for the attack.
- A pipe bomb explodes inside the St Elmo's pizzeria in Camps Bay.

December
- Pagad's Abdus Salaam Ebrahim is arrested in connection with the murder of Rashaad Staggie.

2000

January

- Ayob Mungalee, ex-Pagad member and intelligence informer, implicates one of his former colleagues in the Planet Hollywood bombing.

February

- The State opposes Abdus Salaam Ebrahim's application for bail on the grounds of possible witness intimidation. A police captain claims to know of a witness able to identify Pagad members involved in Bennie Lategan's killing.

May

- Two State witnesses involved in the Lategan murder case and another case concerning an explosion outside the Wynberg Magistrate's Court earlier in the year, are murdered.
- A bomb wrapped in a plastic bag is found on the pavement outside the New York Bagel restaurant in Sea Point. The device is safely defused but, a month later, a car bomb explodes outside the same venue injuring three people.

July

- A bomb explodes at Cape Town International Airport. Director of Public Prosecutions, Bulelani Ncguka, blames Pagad for the blast.

August

- A car bomb explodes outside a coffee shop in the

upmarket Constantia Village shopping complex. Safety and Security Minister, Steve Tshwete, alleges that the bombing is Pagad's response to the arrest of four Pagad members.

- A week later another car bomb is detonated outside The Bronx, a well-known gay night-spot in Green Point.
- Ten days later the third car bomb of the month goes off during the afternoon rush hour on Adderley Street in the heart of Cape Town's CBD.

September
- Wynberg magistrate, Pieter Theron, is killed in the driveway of his Plumstead home. Theron was presiding in several cases involving Pagad members.
- Safety and Security Minister, Steve Tshwete, and Justice Minister, Penuell Maduna, proclaim that Pagad is responsible for the spate of bombings in Cape Town.
- Pagad threatens to seek an interdict restraining them from linking the organisation to the attacks.

October
- So-called Pagad hitman, Ismail Edwards, is sentenced to 25 years for robbery and the attempted murder of alleged drug dealer, Nazeem "Tinkie" Smith.
- The Mhatey brothers (Pagad supporters) are acquitted on charges of possessing explosives.

Their acquittal is attributed to poor police investigative work.

- Pagad's national coordinator, Abdus Salaam Ebrahim, is charged with terrorism under the old Internal Security Act.
- Press reports of the trial of the four men accused of bombing a Wynberg synagogue in 1998 feature evidence from a National Intelligence Agency informer about the activities of the Grassy Park "cell" of Pagad's armed wing, or G-Force.

    Reports say that G-Force members are facing a total of more than 40 charges of murder.

Obviously I was unaware of these undercurrents swirling about in Cape Town the night I set out for the restaurant.

Since the Pagad members have been arrested and brought to trial, the bombings have stopped.

I have reached my own conclusions; you are entitled to yours.

Below is another report, entitled "Patterns of Global Terrorism, 1995–2000," compiled by the US State Department:

Qibla
Description

Qibla is a small South African Islamic extremist group led by Achmad Cassiem, who was inspired by Iran's Ayatollah Khomeini. Cassiem founded Qibla in the 1980s, seeking to establish an Islamic state in South Africa. Pagad began in 1996 as a community anticrime group fighting drug lords in Cape Town's Cape Flats section.

Pagad now shares Qibla's anti-Western stance as well as some members and leadership. Though each group is distinct, the media often treat them as one. Both use front names including Muslims Against Global Oppression (Mago) and Muslims Against Illegitimate Leaders (Mail) when launching anti-Western campaigns.

Activities

Qibla and Pagad routinely protest against US policies toward the Muslim world and use radio station 786 to promote their message and mobilise Muslims.

Pagad is suspected in the car-bombing on 1 January of the Victoria and Alfred Waterfront in Cape Town and the firebombing of a US-affiliated restaurant on 8 January. Pagad is also believed to have masterminded the bombing on 25 August 1998 of the Cape Town Planet Hollywood.

Strength

Qibla is estimated at 250 members. Police estimate there are at least 50 gunmen in Pagad, and the size of Pagad-organized demonstrations suggests it has considerably more adherents than Qibla.

Location/Area of Operation

Operate mainly in the Cape Town area, South Africa's foremost tourist venue.

External Aid

Probably have ties to Islamic extremists in the Middle East.

CHAPTER IV

BEGINNINGS

I was a bully's dream. Small, effeminate and with acne on my face. Bullies just could not resist me. During my entire school career hardly a day went by without me having to deal with these thugs.

One ritual that remains with me even now is this:

The high school I went to was for boys only in a working class neighborhood south of Durban. It was on a hill and at the end of the school day I would have to walk down this hill to get home. Invariably, the bullies lay in wait for me somewhere along that road.

I very quickly realised it was useless to attempt to run away from them or to find an alternative route. They were bigger, stronger and faster than me. So, with resigned anticipation I would approach them. The ritual was always the same. They would remove my school blazer, which my poor mother had sweated blood and tears to purchase and fling it into the highest branch of a nearby tree. Next my school tie would be removed and my hands bound to the tree. My school bag would then be emptied into the garden of a convenient home. All the while I was subjected to taunts, "Sissy, nancy boy, moffie, poof" and I would be hit, jabbed and generally roughed up.

I soon learnt that bullies have a finite attention span, and they would quickly tire of their little game and move off in search of more fulfilling gratification. I would then set about retrieving my possessions. I knew that I dared not arrive home without my prized blazer. So I would scale the tree and retrieve it. Next I would befriend the dog in the garden before venturing in to gather my books, pens, papers and whatnot that had been emptied from my bag. Once I was sure I had gathered all my things I would continue my journey home.

I was but a child and these things hurt. Many a day I would get home, close myself in my bedroom and cry. But this incident and many others like it did not turn me into a "basket case". On the contrary, they served to strengthen my resolve. I learnt to become completely self-contained. "No expectations, no disappointments," became my personal motto – a motto that has remained with me to this day. I decided that I would show these thugs what

I was made of, that I would succeed in life and that nothing they did to me would alter this determination.

I was born in August 1953, the eldest son of Ned and Noreen Walsh. This was Noreen's second marriage and she also had a daughter, from her first marriage. So I came into this world with a sister, Dorothy, eight years my senior. Four years later a brother, Garth, was born.

Despite the four-year gap in our ages, our mother had the bizarre habit of dressing us identically. This endured throughout our childhood. The very first pair of long pants ever purchased for each of us was a pair of powder-blue jeans. We were always together. In fact Noreen never allowed either of us to go anywhere without the other.

This of course changed drastically as we moved into our teens. I was small and not very well liked, with few friends. Garth was the opposite. Taller and bigger than me, he was a surfer and very popular with the boys and girls. He began to lead a great social life and over weekends he was never at home.

Although we drifted apart in those teen years, we re-established a solid and close relationship later on into adulthood. The bomb has simply served to strengthen that closeness. Today Garth, his wife Shelley and their three children are an integral part of my life.

We were a family of five. We lived in a small council house and living with us was our maternal grandmother. It was my grandmother in my childhood years whom I looked to for comfort and love. Like my mother, she was a saleslady and worked in a department store in Durban.

I used to wait at the bus stop every evening for her and as she stepped off the bus she would embrace me proudly in full view of the other commuters. We would then set off up the road hand in hand, with me having relieved her of any parcels she may have had. She always brought home a little treat for Garth and I.

After dinner she and I would settle down in her bedroom and listen to our favourite radio serials on Springbok Radio. No TV in those days. Those evenings were such safe, happy and carefree ones for me. Our warm and loving relationship endured until the day she died.

She eventually went to live in a retirement home in the city and when I was teaching nearby I would make the time to fetch her and treat her to her favourite, an ice cream cone. On pension day, we would have dinner together. She was a very special person.

My father worked as an unskilled artisan in the steel reinforcing industry and my mother held various jobs, from saleslady in a department store to bottle store assistant, butchery assistant and finally a clerk in the motor industry.

Our family was not what would be described as a functional, happy one. My parents either hated passionately or loved passionately. There was no happy, consistent medium. Either way there was little room for the children.

My father did not consider fatherhood a responsibility. And because he enjoyed his drink, weekends, and particularly Friday nights, were very unpleasant. Especially for me.

My father received his wages on a Friday and from bitter experience my mother learned that if she did not wait for him at the factory gate she could kiss the money goodbye. So every Friday I was rounded up and packed into the car to meet Ned at the factory gate.

But he soon got wise to having his wife and son meet him and remove his wages, which prevented his drinking with his mates. He would find other ways of getting out of the factory gates and my mother and I would be left waiting in vain in the growing darkness.

When this happened we would not give up and simply go back home. Oh no, not Noreen Walsh. With me in tow, my angry mother would then trawl the local bars. Bars in those days were "men only" domains. I would have to wait at the entrance and desperately ask a passing waiter or patron whether my father was there.

Amid much mirth and great humour (and for me what seemed like an eternity), I would be told that he had already left or if I was lucky that he was there and he would be out shortly. This message I conveyed to my mother, and we would either wait for him in the car or drive on to the next bar and repeat the process.

This was a humiliating and degrading experience for me, knowing full well that the Friday night would end in some form of friction between my parents. The degree of friction would set the tone for the remainder of the weekend.

But it was not all gloom and doom during this time. My mother's sister and her family lived to the north of Durban in what we spoke of as "a very posh suburb". My aunt would invite Garth and me to spend part of our school holidays with our cousins. I found these breaks away from home really enjoyable.

I was able to forget about the strife at home and whether my father had come home drunk, and what time he had arrived home. I was able to forget about how my mother was coping and whether she had someone to assist her or support her. These visits to my cousins allowed me to become a child again.

It was always with a heavy heart that I returned home at the end of the holidays.

At home too, I devised my own form of escapism. I joined the local library, and soon became an Enid Blyton fan. I would get home from school, and do my homework immediately. When I had finished I would make myself a thick, sweet sandwich and escape to my bedroom where I would devour my Enid Blyton adventure stories.

When I was in Standard 3 an out-of-the-ordinary thing happened. One day my mother arrived home from work with a gift for me. It was a poem. This was unusual because literature was not very high on our family agenda. She sat me down and read it to me. The poem was *If* by Rudyard Kipling, and it was printed on a wall hanging.

At the time I did not really understand the content of the poem. When she had finished she hugged me close to her, and cried. It was an emotional experience to see my mother so moved by the words of this poem. I never forgot that experience.

It was almost as though my mother was aware of what lay ahead for me on my life's journey. It was an almost prophetic moment.

As a result this poem has remained with me to this day and often I refer to it and it has, in a sense, become my mantra.

This is the poem:

If you can keep your head when all about you
Are losing theirs and blaming it on you,
If you can trust yourself when all men doubt you,
But make allowance for their doubting, too;
If you can wait and not be tired by waiting,
Or being lied about, don't deal in lies,
Or being hated don't give way to hating,
And yet don't look too good, nor talk too wise:
If you can dream and not make dreams your master;
If you can think and not make thoughts your aim,

If you can meet with Triumph and Disaster
And treat those two imposters just the same;
If you can bear to hear the truth you've spoken
Twisted by knaves to make a trap for fools,
Or watch the thing you gave your life to broken,
And stoop and build 'em up with worn out tools:
If you can make one heap of all your winnings;
And risk it on one turn of a pitch and toss,
And lose, and start again at your beginnings
And never breathe a word about your loss;
If you can force your heart and nerve and sinew
To serve your turn long after they are gone,
And so hold on when there is nothing in you
Except the Will which says to them "Hold on!"
If you can talk with crowds and keep your virtue,
Or walk with Kings – nor lose the common touch,
If neither foes nor loving friends can hurt you,
If all men count with you, but none too much;
If you can fill the unforgiving minute
With sixty seconds' worth of distance to run,
Yours is the Earth and everything that's in it,
And – which is more – you'll be a Man, my son."

It was only much later that I revisited the poem and truly understood its content.

My troubles at school continued because I had come to the local government school from a Catholic convent, and it was thought that education standards at the convent were higher. So I was placed in the "A" class, but battled to keep up. I very quickly earned the scorn and ridicule of my classmates and the following year I was promoted to the next standard but this time I found myself in the "C" class.

This battle with school work continued until I reached Standard 7, where for the first time a concerned teacher realised that I was emotionally and academically not ready for the level I was in.

I had started school at the age of four, turning five in August of my first school year. So here I was at the end of my year in Standard 7 being told that I had to make a choice: either continue and battle academically for the remainder of my school career or repeat the year in the correct age group for that year.

I don't remember getting much advice or guidance from my parents but the concerned teacher suggested that it would be in my interests to repeat the year, particularly if I wished to obtain a tertiary education.

Fortunately I chose to repeat the year and from then onwards I would always be in at least the top four of the class. It was my academic success that eventually earned me some respect, albeit grudging, as we moved towards matric.

The taunting and teasing and the bullying continued throughout, but in the classroom they were slightly more cautious with me.

Growing up in this rough and tough environment taught me one very useful lesson. That lesson was that I became "streetwise" at a very young age.

I was small and not physical at all and so the

usual methods of defence, fist fighting and other forms of physical violence simply did not work for me. I had to develop techniques that kept me at least one step ahead of my detractors.

I reached matric in the early 1970s and a major topic of conversation among the class in that year was the army. This was still the time of compulsory conscription during which all white South African males had to spend a period of time doing military service.

Talk revolved around how to ensure being posted to the most convenient army camp to home, how to avoid the military altogether, or any other plan that could be employed to "jippo" (cheat) the army.

I had decided that I was going to get this irritation out of the way as soon as possible, and in those days the conscription was for a period of nine months. Rumours abounded that this period was to be increased to a full year. I had no intention of spending a year doing military service so I elected to go to the army directly from school.

So it was that I found myself on a train full of strangers bound for the 1st South African Infantry Battalion, which was then based in Oudtshoorn in the southern Cape. We took what seemed forever to get there, and I was apprehensive about what lay ahead. I was also concerned about my mother being without me for the next nine months and generally very sad and downhearted.

I was not very sporty and anxious about the

physical activity that awaited me. Everyone knew then that as a "troepie" one was in for a tough physical time.

I knew nothing about weapons of any kind or about their maintenance either, and this was to become a turning point for me.

In Oudtshoorn we soon settled into a routine of mindless physical activity. Running, marching, physical exercises and the most boring military lectures. The lectures that I most certainly did not pay much attention to were the ones where we were taught to maintain our rifles.

The day arrived when we were given the chance to practise what we had been taught. The excitement in the camp was tangible. Early in the morning we set out in platoon formation in full kit to the Swartberg Mountain shooting range. We had to jog there, but for most the energy levels were high and the anticipation was great so the distance seemed short. I simply went with the flow, not knowing what to expect.

At the range we faced the target, and were ordered to: "In your own time and at your own target; fire". I braced myself, closed my eyes and fired. The sign came from the target pit that I had missed altogether. I tried again. I pulled the trigger, but nothing happened. The sergeant major standing nearby strode over and took my rifle, and looked down the barrel. There was silence, and then his face turned crimson. "No bloody wonder! This thing hasn't been cleaned since Noah. It is bloody rusty and has never seen oil."

He then demanded to know from me what I thought I was doing and why had I not cleaned and oiled my rifle.

This was just too much for me. I had endured this entire army experience alone. I had not shared my fears, concerns or anxieties with anybody else. I barely had a person to speak to, except for my mother whom I called on Sundays.

Now here I was being shouted at by a larger than life male authority figure, in front of the entire company, who was demanding an explanation. I knew that if I opened my mouth to speak I would burst into tears. The sergeant major took my silence as insubordination, and became even more insistent that I explain. I had to say something.

As I opened my mouth to speak all that emerged was an anguished cry. The tears rolled and I sobbed. The poor sergeant major, I think, had never experienced this before and was not too sure how to handle it. He called a lieutenant over and instructed him to take me away and show me how to clean and oil my rifle. The lieutenant gently led me away and helped me.

After this incident that sergeant major never forgot who I was, and when the day finally arrived for me to go home, I had successfully completed a military officer's intelligence course, and obtained the rank of corporal.

As I was about to climb aboard the army truck taking us to the station, and freedom, he said to me: "The army at least made you a man, hey Walsh!"

It was with pride and a degree of assertiveness that I could reply: "Yes, it did, sergeant major".

The time in the army was a watershed for me. Directly after that unfortunate rifle range incident, I had a long and hard think about the army and me. This passive resistance was doing me no good. I was allowing the army to achieve what the bullies were never able to: to break me.

This thought gave me a jolt. I was becoming a victim to the control of the army. I decided: this far and no further. I was going to change my attitude and I was going to manage the army process and not allow it to control me.

Once this decision had been made things changed. I set myself goals, like for instance, getting fitter on a daily basis, not to be in the last five when having to do a running task, and maximising on every learning opportunity presented.

I learnt to clean my rifle and to at least hit the target when shooting. I began to take charge, looking at things as challenges and not obstacles. With this new attitude time passed rapidly and before I knew it I was heading home, with a newfound confidence. It was this approach, learnt in the army, to take charge and to manage my reaction to my environment that stood me in very good stead later in my life when I was confronted with my biggest challenge.

On returning home I vowed that I was not going to perpetuate my working-class roots. I knew the only way to achieve this was to get a post-matric education.

My academic results were not good enough for me to apply for a university bursary, but they certainly were sufficient for a bursary to study at a teacher's training college. I got a bursary to attend the Edgewood Teacher's College in Pinetown, KwaZulu Natal.

I had three uneventful years at Edgewood, keeping a low profile. I did not belong to any sports clubs or social groups. Instead I focused on my studies and kept to myself.

From Standard 8, I had always managed to get part-time work, over weekends and during holidays. I worked in shoe shops, bottle stores, restaurants and even for a bookmaker.

This continued while I was a student teacher. I do not remember ever having a real break. When I wasn't studying, I was working. From my first year at college I was not in any way dependent on my parents. My bursary paid for my tuition and the money I earned kept me in pocket money.

I am a Catholic and throughout my childhood my faith remained a constant for me.

So it was, I think, a natural progression once I had graduated to want to teach in a Catholic school. This goal was achieved when I was appointed as a brand new teacher at St Henry's College in Durban.

At the time the staff was a mixture of lay teachers

and Marist Brothers and the ethos of the school was exactly what I had expected. Very soon I fitted in comfortably. I involved myself in every facet of the school and was coaching junior rugby and cricket.

One of the Brothers became a good friend and it was due to his influence that I took up road running and began to play squash. The running was done earnestly and to my surprise I actually enjoyed it.

I also found that it was good therapy. When I needed to sort issues out I was able to do so while running. I played squash with a similar passion. I got quite good at it.

In my third year at the school I began to get restless and I realised that I was not content with just a teacher's diploma. I wanted a university education and to experience life on a university campus. Life had more to offer than being a teacher.

So after three happy years at St Henry's, I resigned and moved on.

In 1980 I was teaching in Johannesburg as a stop gap when I saw an advert in the *Sunday Times*. It was a mining company offering bursaries to people wanting to study a Social Science degree at a university.

I jumped at the chance and after a series of interviews I was awarded a bursary. The University of the Witwatersrand beckoned, and in 1982 I found myself a full-time student again.

This time I was much older than the others in my class, but this did not bother me. If anything, it worked to my advantage. I was more mature and I was able to use my past experience constructively to make my university experience really enjoyable.

I also managed to find a part-time teaching job to bring in some extra money.

I had had a solid Christian grounding as a child. Church was central to our lives and I think it was something that sustained us as we grew up in the somewhat dysfunctional environment we did.

It was at this stage of my life that I began to move away from my Christian roots.

It was ironic in a sense because I was teaching at a religious Jewish school where God was central to their existence and it was while I was at this school that I drifted further and further away from my beliefs. It was not because of the school that this happened.

Rather, I began to find that with my newfound self-confidence and my pimple-free face (for the first time in my adult life) as well as the fact that I was a jogger, played squash and had joined the gym, people began to find me attractive.

I was able to choose the person I wanted to take out to dinner, and when invited they accepted. This was a whole new concept to me, something I enjoyed. It gave me a sense of power.

But I remained wary of people and very seldom let them into my personal space. I learnt that people like to talk about themselves and I quickly developed the social skill of asking questions about the people with whom I interacted. In this way they did the talking, and seldom got the opportunity to ask about me.

So I appeared to be this interested, caring person but in fact it was a defence mechanism that I used to great effect. In my later career it became a very useful tool.

In all this time I was unable to develop any long-term relationships. They were short lived and without wanting to sound vain, I think many people were hurt by my approach. I am not proud of the fact that I played with other people's emotions in the manner I did, but my mindset at the time was, "No expectations, no disappointments". This was a philosophy that I firmly believed in and I expected others to adhere to it as well.

One of the bursary conditions was that during varsity vacations I had to work in the personnel department of one of the company mines. This experience made me decide that after graduation I was not going to work on a mine.

In 1984 I graduated with a BA degree, majoring in Industrial Sociology and Clinical Psychology. This was one of my proudest moments. Neither my parents nor any member of my family attended the ceremony, but some of my closest friends did.

Having made the decision not to honour my bursary commitments, I was left with the onerous task of repaying the study funds, so finding a job was foremost in my mind. A newly graduated person with limited experience is not a desirable commodity in the job market.

But my teaching experience was what I traded on. My first appointment was as a training officer in the manufacturing industry. I was appointed primarily to conduct supervisory development training. The fact that I had never supervised a single person in the work environment before never crossed my mind. I took the job because it paid well and it gave me a car to drive.

It was a disaster. I was expected to manage a team of people, never having done so before, and to teach concepts that I barely understood, let alone had experienced.

I was unhappy and so too were my employers with my work performance. Very soon, under the pretext of a departmental restructuring, I was offered a severance package.

I took the package with great relief and fled. For a period in the mid 1980s I had a series of ill-suited jobs. With the benefit of hindsight, this can be attributed to the fact that I took the jobs offered to me for all the wrong reasons.

Instead of having a clear career plan, knowing in which sector I felt comfortable and what my competencies were, I chased instead a job for the salary and the car as well as the status it offered. I was invariably appointed to positions for which I clearly was not suited to from a competence and experience point of view. Very quickly the "Peter Principle" came into play and I would find an excuse to leave the position and move on. The result was that I got little job satisfaction, made very little contribution to the business and both the employer and I were unhappy with the situation.

It was during this period that I began to develop a taste for the finer things in life. Fancy homes, fast cars, and generally living the life of a hedonist.

But at the same time because of my lack of career satisfaction and general unhappiness in the working environment I began to think the problem was that I was simply lazy and did not want to work.

I found myself looking for any excuse to avoid being physically present at the office. In psychological terms this is called practising "avoidance behaviour". This means that when a person is expected to function in a position beyond their level of competence and they cannot do so, they simply avoid the situation in the hope that it will disappear.

All of this changed, thankfully, in March 1989, when I met the man who was to become my boss for the next three years and who has remained a mentor ever since.

The Standard Bank of South Africa had begun a process of identifying staff who had the potential to develop into senior managers. The bank wished to fast track the development of these people and an Assessment Center was set up to implement the program.

The person appointed to head this project within the Standard Bank was Hilton Blake. Hilton is an industrial psychologist and had been teaching at the University of the Witwatersrand's Business School before joining the bank.

He was looking for two people to assist him in the running and design refinement of the assessment process. He had already appointed one person and was looking for another.

I applied for the position and was given an interview. Hilton has the ability to be intimidating at times and in that initial interview he intimidated me almost into submission.

He asked probing questions and was not overly impressed with my work record. But somewhere, somehow, he must have seen some potential beneath this apparently insecure and directionless person.

After a second interview he offered me the job. I was over the moon and when he told me that the position came with a company car and proceeded to list the makes of car I could choose from I began to see stars.

The list included a BMW 316. At that stage I think I was more excited about the car then about the nature of the job. This soon changed because Hilton was a hard and demanding taskmaster. He has a demanding nature and is a perfectionist where work is concerned, but he also treated me in a nurturing and caring manner.

So it was that for the first time in my working career, since giving up teaching, I found myself in a working environment that was nurturing, supportive, encouraging and empowering. I blossomed here. I enjoyed the work I was doing and I felt a sense of belonging to Standard Bank. I was the

Assessment Center administrator and this entailed running the entire assessment process.

My self-esteem developed along with my confidence and the social skill that I had learnt earlier in life, to ask people to talk about themselves, rather than my having to talk about myself, came to be a very useful tool in the job I was doing.

When Hilton offered me the job, it came with a condition. I only had an undergraduate degree, and he stipulated that within the first two years of working for him I had to obtain a postgraduate qualification.

I naturally agreed to this condition, because I wanted the job, and more especially the BMW. He held me to the agreement. The Wits Business School offered a two-year part-time course in Human Resources Management. I registered for the program and in January 1991 I yet again found myself a student.

I spent the next two years of my life attending lectures, three times a week after hours, and when I wasn't attending lectures I was either working, attending syndicate meetings or completing assignments. It was a busy and demanding time of my life, but also a satisfying time. I thrived and grew in all respects through this process.

By the time we got into our second year my confidence level had increased to the point where I was bold enough to stand for and be elected class representative for that year.

Life was good in the early 1990s. I had a job that I enjoyed immensely, a boss who was interested in my development and I worked in an environment that was stimulating and challenging.

I purchased my first house in Johannesburg and my career had direction. Hilton Blake had taken me in and like an injured bird had nurtured and cared for me. He had challenged and chided me and pointed me in the right direction, and when he saw I was ready to fly, he set me free.

In my third year as a member of Hilton's team, I started getting restless and began looking around the bank for a different and a more demanding challenge. Hilton sensed this and encouraged me to move on.

At this time the bank had opened an operation in Swaziland and was looking for someone to set up a human resources and training function. I applied for the position even though I had never been a human resources practitioner, or been to Swaziland. This did not seem to deter the bank and I got the job and the promotion. This was in keeping with my new found goal focus in life. I wanted to be a human resources practitioner and this was a good oppor-tunity to gain the necessary experience in a short space of time.

When I first went to Swaziland to look over my new working environment and to meet the people I would be working with, the reality of what I was in for hit home hard.

My new boss, who was the antithesis of Hilton Blake, had been against my appointment because of my relative lack of experience. I was then taken on a tour of the working environment and shown my office. Throughout this visit the reality of my decision horrified me and the enormity of the move became greater and greater.

By the end of that day and on the return trip to Johannesburg I was scheming on how I was going to get out of this commitment and to remain in my nice secure post on Hilton's team. This was my comfort zone and I was being wrenched right out of it into a hostile and unfamiliar place.

Further, I had to give up my home and my support group of a few very close and good friends. This reality frightened me and I felt all the insecurities and self-doubt that I hoped I had discarded, creeping back.

The first day back at the office in Johannesburg I announced rather dramatically that I had changed my mind about the Swaziland position. I no longer wanted to go, I announced to the horror and amazement of my superiors. In response I was met with a stony silence and was told in no uncertain terms that my change of mind and emotionally immature behaviour was career-limiting to say the least.

I was eventually persuaded to go to save face and salvage my shattered reputation. So it was with a great sadness that I awaited the arrival of the Elliot's removal truck to move my possessions to Mbabane, Swaziland.

In Mbabane I resolved to make this new job work. I was there on a two-year contract and I decided as I sat, that first night, alone in my new home, that the best way to deal with this is to make the best of the situation and to engross myself in work – and I did.

The relationship with the hostile trade union was normalised, the payroll was computerised and centralised and a training unit was begun. I enjoyed my job and I began to enjoy living in Swaziland.

I was single and most ex-pats my age were married. Nonetheless, I became friends with three young accountants working at the local Southern Sun Hotel complex in the Ezulweni valley. They became my squash partners, my running mates and my drinking buddies.

I had been promoted to take the post in Swaziland, and on my return to Johannesburg I was again promoted to a more senior position, as human resources manager for Standard Bank's central services units.

In Johannesburg, I again established my network of friends and colleagues. I enjoyed my work, the gym and my running. I had been back at head office for almost four years when I was asked to consider taking the provincial human resources job based in Cape Town. I jumped at the opportunity.

I had spent many enjoyable holidays in the Cape and it was always a wish of mine to live there. This was like a dream come true. I was subjected to the usual selection process and eventually I was informed that I was the successful candidate. I was to report as soon as possible. I immediately began to put plans into action. My house was put on to the market, and I began looking for accommodation in Cape Town.

I arrived in Cape Town to start work in my new position, Human Resources Manager, Retail Banking, Western Cape, at the beginning of October 1997. I bought a house with remarkable views over the vineyards of the northern suburbs and everything fell into place as planned. My office had an uninterrupted view of Table Mountain and there was a gym just over the road.

I felt that I had landed a job in heaven. Life quickly settled down to an ordered pace. Work, gym, run, squash. I set about creating a garden in my new home and generally I was quite content with my new life style. I occasionally missed friends and the pace of life left behind in Johannesburg but on the whole life was good. I slowly began to make friends with the Capetonians and to re-establish connections with Johannesburg acquaintances, now living in Cape Town.

A very dear and close friend of mine from Johannesburg had, at about the same time as my move to Cape Town, relocated to George in the Southern Cape. He is a medical doctor, an oncologist. He had moved to George to open an oncology practice there.

Ronald Uijs and I had met many years ago at a mutual friend's birthday party. We quickly became good friends and for many years played squash together, and then we would ruin the good exercise by drinking beer after the squash game. But those were enjoyable years.

We both were keen runners and as members of the Varsity Kudu's club ran many marathons together and in 1986 completed the Comrades marathon. We went on to compete in the Two Oceans marathon together. So with him being only four hours away from Cape Town I soon became familiar with the N2 highway from Cape Town for weekend visits to George.

It was not all wine and roses however, as my work was demanding. With the massive changes taking place in the political landscape of South Africa, the bank was undergoing great change as well. People were uncomfortable and so my job and the work of my department was challenging and at times stressful. But I thrived on the demands of the job and the stress simply enhanced my adrenaline levels. I like to think that at this time of great change in our organisation I played a strong role.

My career was on track and I knew I must make the most of my time in Cape Town in order to advance further up the career ladder. I wanted ultimately to return to Head Office in Johannesburg.

Before I knew it, 19th August 1998 was upon me. It was my 45th birthday. I was attending a leadership development program at the Standard Bank's College in Morningside, Johannesburg at the time.

That evening, a friend and colleague, Francis Sinclair (who was on the same program), and I went out to dinner in a nearby restaurant to celebrate the occasion. We had a pleasant meal together, little knowing that in under a week my life would forever be different. I returned to Cape Town on Friday 21 August. I had a quiet weekend at home with my dogs. I spent the time catching up on issues that had accumulated while I had been away. Monday morning came as usual, all too quickly, and so began what I thought would be another ordinary, busy week at the office.

Bruce was a keen runner and completed many races as well as a Comrades marathon.

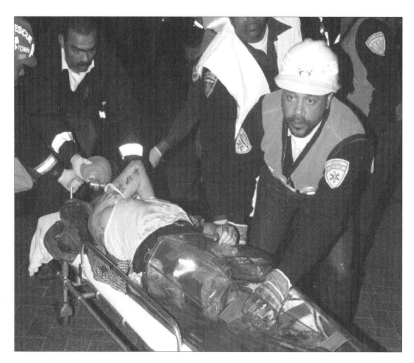

ABOVE: The devastating aftermath of the Planet Hollywood bomb.

BELOW: Bruce in the Somerset Hospital connected to life support systems.

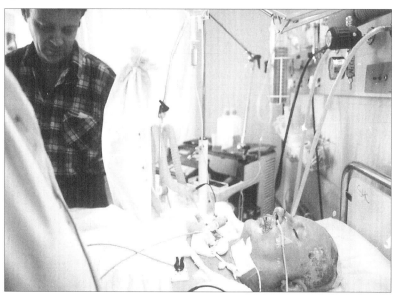

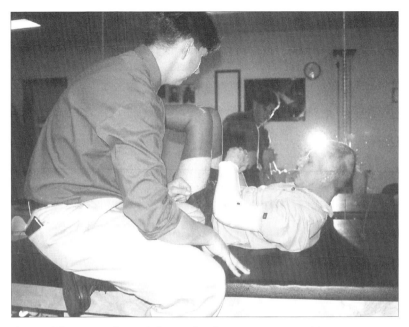

ABOVE: The struggle and determination to get use to his new prosthetic legs.

BELOW: Bruce's first steps on his new legs.

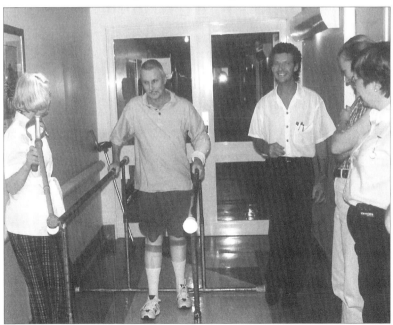

ABOVE: At home, after five weeks in hospital, getting stronger and fitter.

BELOW: Bruce passed his driving test with flying colours in his specially made adapted motorcar.

CHAPTER V

RECOVERY

There I was, unconscious, burnt, bruised and bat-
tered in the intensive care ward of the Somerset
Hospital. The people most important to me, my
brother Garth, my sister Dorothy, my friend Ronald
and my cousin Kelly were all there and slowly but
surely visitors who could afford to and could
make their way to Cape Town, began to stream in
anxiously to see me.

During those first 24 hours that I lay in Somerset Hospital my condition was critical. Nobody
expected me to live. Garth and Dorothy were told
to expect the worst. They waited anxiously while I
was blissfully unaware of what had happened to
me. The core people, namely Garth, Dorothy,

Ronald, Kelly and Carolyn kept a close 24-hour vigil.

When I survived the first 24 hours after the bomb, concern began to creep into the doctors' minds. They had to ascertain whether I had bleeding on the brain and they were concerned that the burst eardrums would leave me deaf. There was also some worry about whether the force of the blast had left me brain damaged.

I was disabled, having lost both my legs, and at that stage they were unsure how effectively I would be able to use my left arm which they had been able, so far, to save.

After I had stabilised at Somerset I was transferred to City Park Hospital where I was moved into the intensive care unit. Doctors told me afterwards that if I had not been so fit I probably would not have made it. So all the marathons and gym sessions did pay off, after all.

In City Park I was in an isolation unit within the intensive care unit – I called it "the little bubble".

My visitors had to look at me through a window and only a selected few were allowed private access and contact. I think the doctors feared that I would be easily infected and kept most people away from me.

I was still unconscious. Then the debate began: How long should they keep the life support machines going? Should they finally switch off the machines and let fate take over? I was still haemorrhaging internally. I was still critical, but stable.

By that time I was being prayed for in churches throughout South Africa. People prayed for me daily. My friend Thomas O'Reilly had organised a priest who gave me the last rites – again unbeknown to be. I lay there totally unaware of the anxiety, the trauma and the stress that was a result of the bomb.

On day 17 the medication to stop the internal bleeding finally kicked in, and I came back to this world. I was conscious again.

But because of the severity of my injuries I was kept heavily sedated.

So while I was conscious and beginning to interact with people who visited me and shared some sort of interest in the activities around me, I didn't at that stage fully absorb the enormity of what had happened to me.

When I look back at that particular time, I have very little memory of who visited me and what was said. Doctors have told me that this was due to a natural reaction from my body and mind, called "post-traumatic amnesia", where memory is blanked out to avoid the stress of facing up to what had happened.

It is still quite embarrassing when people ask me afterwards whether I recall their visits. Although I am grateful that they came to see me, I'm afraid I cannot remember very much, or who exactly came to see me.

Little incidents are still quite clear, though. Garth was particularly concerned that I had some sort of brain damage and every time he saw me, he would hold up fingers in front of my face and ask me: "How many?"

Or he would ask me to do basic subtraction, addition and multiplication sums; and he would ask me the names of various people in the room. Just to test that I was still mentally sound.

The other bit I recall is that friends of mine, Johnny and Amanda Uijs, who live in Brackenfell in the Cape, came to see me one evening. Amanda is a nursing sister, so she was quite comfortable in the intensive care ward but Johnny was not.

He was thoroughly uncomfortable sitting in such an atmosphere with all the dying and gravely sick people around him. When it was time for them to leave, I said to them through the hole in my throat (because the tracheotomy pipe had been removed): "Take me home. This place is evil."

This weird reaction was probably due to a bit of paranoia induced by the quantity of drugs I was still taking. I remember that years before, when I went overseas for the first time, I visited some friends in London.

One night before leaving a night club one of them urged me to take an Ecstasy tablet, and under protest I took half. I danced the night away in the club, but in the early morning hours, paranoia set in.

That was the quick end to my drug experimentation. But funnily enough, the same reaction now kicked in, in the hospital. Heavily sedated as my body fought to recover from the awful damage done to it, I was convinced that I was being held prisoner – held there against my will – and that people were drugging me and keeping me in this state of mind because they wanted to take advantage of my situation.

I could see that this upset Johnny no end as I pleaded with my deep-set eyes, saying: "Please take me home. This place is evil. They are giving me drugs."

What also came through strongly then was a constant desire to go home, to return to my life as before. I wanted a return to normality.

In the days after I regained consciousness I was in a very bad state, emotionally and psychologically.

I constantly nagged one of the doctors – a youngish one called Joe Grobbelaar – to let me go home. I kept saying: "I have to go home. I have to go and see my dogs."

Eventually, in late September, Dr Grobbelaar called my bluff. He said I could go home for exactly one hour on a Saturday under certain conditions.

These were that an intensive care nursing sister; a physiotherapist and Ronald accompany me.

I rallied support from my hospital and one of the sisters gave up her lunch hour to come with me. I bullied the physiotherapist, Clodagh, to come and of course poor Ronald had no option. So when Saturday morning arrived I was bundled into a wheelchair and wrapped up, still in my pyjamas. At this stage I was still sedated and the reality of losing my legs hadn't dawned on me yet. I just wanted to go home.

You can imagine this whole entourage trooping down to my car which was parked in the garage below the hospital.

I was put in the back seat and I remember feeling quite peeved by this. Weird, but I still had not realised that I had no legs. We drove from the City Park Hospital right out to the northern suburbs, to Protea Valley.

It was good to be outside. Fresh air, the sun was shining. The green of plants and trees whizzing by. I was much relieved to see the world again outside of a hospital ward.

But when we arrived at my home, my two dogs Emma, a spaniel, and my SPCA special fox terrier, Flekkie, didn't recognise me. I think I still smelt of burnt flesh and wounds, and they showed no interest in me whatsoever.

This really upset me and the outing had exhausted me. I was so exhausted that I had to lie down.

Poor Ronald had to entertain the physiotherapist and the intensive care nurse while I settled down in my own bed after being away from it for many weeks.

Ronald said that under no circumstances were they returning to the hospital after how much I had moaned, and they were all going to enjoy their break from the hospital and have their full lunch hour.

So, while they had a meal, I lay in my bed. I

remember how lovely it felt to be in my own place; to lie in my own bed and be surrounded by all my own, familiar things. The familiar brings some comfort.

There were pictures of my family members, and my favourite paintings by Frans Claerhout. He is a Belgian Catholic priest who paints African versions of biblical scenes. Under my own duvet, I slept like a baby.

Being home again after weeks in hospital gave me psychological peace of mind.

The hour passed quickly and when I was woken up I was packed into the wheelchair; loaded back into the car and taken back to the hospital. The whole entourage made its way back to City Park.

During this time I was told by several people that I had lost both my legs; that I was now what was known as a "bilateral amputee". But for whatever reason I never really absorbed this fact. I listened and I heard what the people said, I heard what I was told, but it did not sink in. It never really entered my mind that I had actually lost my legs.

It did just not register.

People became concerned about my almost nonchalant reaction to this horrific condition. People would remark how well I was coping – how well I was dealing with it.

But Ronald knew the truth. "Wait," he told people. "He hasn't yet absorbed it. It hasn't hit home just yet. When he does, we must be there to pick up the pieces."

When I was eventually moved out of the intensive care ward to a general ward the nurse orderly pushing me in my wheelchair said: "You know, when people usually come out of this little bubble we take them straight to the mortuary."

I remember jokingly telling to her to make sure that I was going to the ward – not the mortuary!

I now had a little private ward to myself with a view of the mountain. It was pleasant, cheerful and chirpy with the hospital staff, visitors, and all and sundry who came to see me. It seemed as though I was getting along fine.

The irony of the situation was that I had no idea that I had no legs.

I was even less aware of what had happened to my arm. The impact of the blast had shattered the bones. My arm looked like something out of a sci-fi movie, with an exo-skeleton attached to the outside. Doctors were hoping that the bones would regrow.

Although I had been told there were metal rods going through my left arm, I really, really didn't absorb the enormity of my situation.

But one day reality intruded upon my world. It was towards the end of September, about a month after the blast.

Morning. The sun was rising and I looked out of the hospital window and I wondered where I was. I thought to myself: "This is not where I should be. This isn't my bed."

I did not recognise the view and I didn't recognise the bed. My first impression was that it must have been one hell of a party that I had been to the night before, because this was not where I was supposed to be. Strange what tricks one's mind can play.

I thought to myself that it was time for me to get up; find my clothes; find my car and get home.

I was blissfully unaware that I was connected to a battery of machinery behind me, but I knew that I needed to get up.

I struggled to get out of bed, but if you do not have legs, you do not get very far. I crashed onto the hospital floor. The poor ward sister came rushing in.

"Please, Bruce," she said. "You have enough cuts and bruises. You don't have to go and cut your head open." I remember saying to her very vividly, very clearly, through this hole in my throat: "Where am I? What's happened?"

And it was the weirdest, weirdest feeling to be told that Fanie Schoeman, who had been a colleague for so long and with whom I had worked so closely the last few months, was dead and buried. And Brian Duddy, dead and gone as well.

And then she told me what the bomb had done to me. She did so very gently, very clearly and with great empathy. When she had finished I asked to be left alone.

She closed the curtains across the window, and discreetly placed the bell within my reach. The door closed softly.

I lay still and stared at the ceiling, desperately trying to make sense of everything she had told me. I lay there thinking: This can't be true. This can't have happened to me. It is all a bad dream.

Eventually I screwed up some courage and, with difficulty, raised myself in the bed.

Slowly I lifted the sheets. Where my legs should have been, there was nothing – just a white sheet, and two stumps. That was reality.

I stared for a moment in disbelief and slowly my disbelief turned to horror at the enormity of my loss.

My first reaction was to cry, to cry deeply. Not gentle tears, but tears of rage, loss, of helplessness and despair. Raw animal noises came from my mouth.

I have never experienced such shock, horror, disbelief. I could not believe that this was my body.

You know, I had a good pair of legs. I ran marathons, played squash. I thought they were magnificent, and they were a part of me. Now they were gone.

Running was always so therapeutic, I really enjoyed it. I used to push myself, test my own boundaries when I ran. I did not race against others, but against myself. Always a better time, a longer distance.

As the pain of realisation subsided, I knew that I could not lie there, crying for the rest of my life. I had to do something.

And I remember thinking: These 'bliksems'. They can take my legs and they can take my colleagues. But what I will *not* do is give the planters of this bomb the satisfaction that they have taken a full life from me. I was going to fight to get that back.

In hindsight, I think that was a somewhat naive decision to have made, but a decision that I took nonetheless. I did not realise what lay ahead, and the struggle it would require to reclaim my full life.

I thought they would fit me with a new pair of plastic legs, and life would be just dandy again – it would be no different. I thought I could simply reverse the clock to before the bomb and be the old Bruce again.

A snap of the fingers and the loss was gone. I did not realise then that I would have to make a new life for myself, and deal with the damage wrought on my body – and my mind.

By this time Garth and Dorothy had returned to Durban. They had jobs to go to and families to support. Ronald had also returned to George, but came to visit regularly.

Whenever I saw anybody that I cared for: Carolyn, Kelly, or any of my colleagues, Ronald, I cried … I cried a lot. But there was also a determination within me to overcome. I never even vaguely contemplated using a wheelchair. It was simply not an option.

I also decided that I would need the help of a psychologist to overcome the emotional scars. As I had done a degree in psychology, I knew that I would choose my psychologist carefully and not see just anyone.

So there followed a procession of "shrinks" through my ward whom I interviewed for the job. I knew that I would try to dominate any counsellor, so I chose carefully, and selected Linda Kantor.

While I chose a psychologist to sort out my mind, the hospital arranged for someone to sort out a pair of new legs for me.

A ward sister told me that Stefan Kritzinger would be arriving that day to measure me for my legs. She said he was one of the best in South Africa and that I should trust him.

Stefan duly arrived – he was a young, open-faced guy. I immediately liked him. He was very sensitive to one's needs and emotions.

I will always remember his approach with gratitude. He was clever. He arrived that first day with an example of what my legs would look like – the full ensemble, even down to the toes and toe nails.

"I will make your legs look so real," he said, "that you will wear sandals on your feet." And he gave me a pair of sandals.

He had managed to find a photo somewhere of my feet and said he would copy them exactly for me.

It was a great ploy. If Stefan had arrived with just the aluminium rods that the legs are constructed from, I don't know how I would have reacted. I would probably have gone nuts.

So Stefan took measurements, coming back once or twice for alterations.

How they make a prosthesis is to make a plaster of paris mould around what is left of your legs, the rods are attached to plastic, or silicone feet, and the legs are then built up.

A few days later he was back with my new legs. One rolls a silicon sleeve onto the stump and at the base is a pin which then clicks into the prosthesis.

I remember looking at them and thinking – so, these are going to be my new means of transport.

On the first day when he fitted them, I tentatively stood, holding on and clutching for dear life to everything and everyone.

Up to this point the physiotherapists had kept me exercised lying in bed, lifting my arms, lifting what was left of my legs, doing stomach exercises and so on.

This was near the end of September, about six weeks after the blast.

My arm still hosted the exo-skeleton, and my left hand was in a brace. The nerves that should control my hand and arm had been severed and the hand was still limp, hanging like a dead fish in front of me.

Most of my burns had healed but scars on my back still needed tending to every day.

Stefan had also been to see Matty Duddy, who was in the same hospital.

It was quite an occasion when both of us emerged from our rooms for our first walk.

Matty's two children were there for her, and Carolyn for me. Stefan, the ward sisters and nurses and all the physios made up quite an audience.

I was wheeled out of my room in a wheelchair, and I strapped on my new legs. I was helped up, and took hold of the bars that had been fastened to the passage wall outside our rooms.

I held on for dear life while taking the first tentative steps, and "walked" for about five metres to the resounding cheers of the audience. Turning around was hell.

Each successful step was greatly applauded, and encouraged with "Come on Bruce – you can do it." I owe that nursing staff a lot.

It was difficult to learn to balance on these new contraptions, and the prosthesis was very heavy to move forward. I felt really vulnerable and spread my legs wide, like a cowboy, to keep upright.

Matty received a similar cheer all around when she strapped on her one new leg and wobbled along.

While I was trying out my new legs, getting used to them and learning how to walk properly on them, I was battling to control my mind and my emotions.

I was angry and sad at the same time. All these negative emotions seemed to merge into one. I would often lie in my hospital bed and say I didn't want to live any more.

I saw others walking, running outside, whole human beings.

My legs, the Comrades marathon, playing squash – all these things were gone forever.

This – these two stumps – was my new reality. I was really battling with my left hand as well, and could only use my right hand to help me do anything.

They were dark, dark days, those days in September 1998.

As the days wore on I set into a routine. I had graduated from having bed baths to being taken to the bathroom and bathed. I also very quickly decided who I would allow to bath me and who I wouldn't.

I was embarrassed by my broken and scarred body – I did not want people to see me. The only people I felt comfortable with were an older nurse, and a very sensitive male nurse.

So my days began to unfold to a typical routine: breakfast was served at some ungodly hour and I would moan and complain about being woken up soon after I had fallen asleep. Doctor's rounds followed and medication was handed out; nurses would visit me; my dressings would be changed; physiotherapists would then exercise me in bed.

By the time I graduated to putting my legs on and walking on the parallel bars in the passage, it was lunch-time. After that visitors arrived and that spilled over into the evening.

There was a core of regular visitors, and Carolyn Stewart was the leader of the pack. During this time we developed a very close bond and friendship which has endured to this day. It was at this stage towards the end of September that I decided that I needed to re-look at my spiritual existence and so I requested to see a priest. I wanted to see a Catholic priest, because I was, after all, a lapsed Catholic.

One morning there was a rather anxious knock on my door and this young priest peeked around the edge of the door.

He introduced himself as Father Hugh, and said that he believed that I wanted to see him.

We had a very rewarding talk and that set a path to my spiritual reawakening.

Meanwhile I was making steady progress and my recovery was looking good, so it was decided that I could go home. I was eventually discharged in the first week of October 1998, after spending nearly two months in hospital.

I decided that I would go home alone, much to the consternation of my friends and family.

Their concerns proved to be on the ball, because at home it was quite a battle to cope on my own.

But I wanted my independence back – and my privacy. I was not prepared to give up the two things in life that I valued most highly, and was determined to overcome any obstacle to regain them.

A typical day would be for me to move myself from my bed into a wheelchair and then have a bath.

Carolyn would arrive to change the dressings on my legs and back. I still had extensive burn wounds on my back as well.

At that stage my legs, or what was left of them, were still very tender and sore. It takes some adaptation to have them socketed into the prosthesis for long periods.

This continued well into November, with doctors urging me to spend as much time as possible wearing the prosthesis.

They said this would force the stumps to take on the shape of the sleeve that they sat in.

I still had problems with my breathing and the debris from the bomb which had damaged my lungs. So included in the round of medical personnel visiting would be a ear, nose and throat specialist. I also had dizzy spells from the inner ear damage, which made getting used to my new legs quite a task. After Carolyn had been there the physiotherapist would arrive and then my psychologist.

My home was sometimes like Grand Central station, with people, phone calls, flowers, and fruit pouring through. Although I had an absolute appreciation for the care people showed, sometimes it actually became too much.

In the evenings I could at last shut the door on the world and retire quietly, but sometimes being alone at night would be overwhelming.

As I lay in my own bed with my dogs on either side of me (by this time my dogs had got to know me again) I would very often feel very, very sorry for myself and I would cry.

Certain things would set me off. I would lie in my bed and look at my shower and think I would never again be able to stand and have a shower.

I would look out on the road and see people jogging by and think, that never again would I be able to do that, and that would set me off. And I would look at my bruised, broken and damaged body and the tears would flow.

Running was my therapy. That is what I did when I needed to sort things out. On those sturdy legs of mine I attempted three Comrades Marathons, and finished one. I also ran the Two Oceans.

I did these races because I could. It was a test for me. I did not know how to replace that part of my life, and as a result felt greatly diminished.

Word got out that I was alone at home in the evenings and that I would get into these depressed moods, so it was decided that I should get a night nurse. I will never forget what happened: the poor night nurse arrived to start her duties one Sunday afternoon at about about five o'clock (I think she worked from 17:00 in the afternoon until 07:00 the next morning.)

She had just got there and was beginning to settle down and find out what it was that she had to do, when I decided that I didn't need a night nurse and certainly didn't want her in my house.

I called her into my room and I said: "What is the fee? How much did it cost you to get here? Here's the money. Off you go please, I don't want you to be here so don't bother to come back."

And off she went (I think quite relieved that she didn't have to spend the evening there) and the very next day I contacted the nursing agency and said: "Thank you very much, I don't think I need the services of a night nurse."

But pressure was put on me. I couldn't live alone. It was just not feasible. What would happen in an emergency? How would I get out of the house if there was any danger? Eventually I was persuaded that I needed to get someone, and so I contacted the mother of a friend of mine who was now living in New Zealand.

Aubrey Welsh and I had come a long way from the days that we were students at Edgewood College together and I had become good friends with Aubrey's mother, Tilly, who lived in Durban.

Garth got involved and persuaded me to contact her. I called her and said: "Tilly, please come and look after me in Cape Town."

Without hesitation she gave up her life in Durban and was soon with me in Cape Town, where she took over running the house.

She organised the visitors every day, fed them, served them refreshments, and looked after me.

Between Tilly and Carolyn they made my days. I was looked after and it was an absolute privilege for me to have someone like Tilly around all the time – at my beck and call. And I think I was not exactly the easiest person to be around. I was quite demanding; quite obnoxious at times, I think, and quite rude – but Tilly endured it all. She was there through thick and thin.

The time eventually arrived in late October when I decided that I now wanted to see my brother and my sister. They had last seen me shortly after the bomb blast, and would recall the state of mind and condition I was in. I wanted them to come and visit again and see the progress I had made.

Garth's wife was heavily pregnant at this time, and about to give birth. Garth and Dorothy (or Billy as we call her) arrived some time in October and I think they were both pleasantly surprised to see the progress I had made, but I could see the hurt and the sadness in their eyes when they looked at their brother.

One evening Kelly was also due for a visit so we decided to have a braai. There must have been about six or seven of us. Ronald, me, Garth, Billy, Kelly and Kelly's friend, Maggie. We had a lovely braai. I was still wheelchair bound, not being very mobile in my prostheses and only putting them on for a few minutes a day at that stage.

We were sitting outside and while we were busy braaiing, I suddenly felt a bit cold and so I asked to be taken inside. Ronald very nonchalantly decided he would bring me in. When we got to the door from the veranda into the dining room there is a little step and instead of tilting the wheelchair backwards, he tilted it forwards as he was trying to lift the wheelchair over the step.

I came out of the chair like a bag of potatoes, falling to the ground on my stump, particularly on my right stump, which was in any event quite painful. I can remember crying in absolute frustration and with pain and humiliation and I insisted that I wanted to go to my room to lie down for a while.

But Garth was not having any of this. He came into my room and told me in no uncertain terms that I had a commitment to my visitors and that I couldn't just lie in my bed feeling sorry for myself. I had to join in and be part of the dinner, because after all that was why everybody was there.

And so with great difficulty and great discomfort and certainly in great pain I reappeared in the dining room to sit and have my meal with my visitors.

That fall was the start of a process where I discovered that I had an abscess in my right stump. The stump was painful, but everybody told me that this was due to being forced to get used to the shape of the prosthesis.

At no stage did anyone even think that I could have an abscess. It was only weeks afterwards that that Ronald had a closer look and found the abscess. He lanced it and a lot of gunge came out.

But the pain didn't subside. It persisted. Eventually, I went to see the orthopaedic surgeon who had worked with me while I was still in hospital and he found that the abscess had reappeared.

Still the pain persisted and eventually in November I was hospitalised yet again in the City Park Hospital where he had to cut open my stump under anaesthetic to determine what it was that was causing the discomfort.

It transpired that the wax initially put into the wound when they were amputating the leg had not dissolved, as it should have done. This wax was causing the infection. Once it was removed, and once the wound had healed, I was able to take to my prosthesis with great delight – certainly with a greater delight than ever before that point.

At this time I was also introduced to a wonderful lady called Sue, an occupational physiotherapist. When I met her, her very first words were: "Bruce, I'll teach you to manage your disability." And those words I have never forgotten.

Once she told me that, I decided there and then that I was going to learn to manage my disability and at no stage allow my disability to ever manage me. It was Sue who taught me to be mobile around the house and who would help me to get in and out of the bath and on and off toilets and how to do things independently of other people.

It was also Sue who told me that I needed to obtain a disabled driver's licence. Sue made the arrangements and at the end of November I was on my way for my driving test.

At this stage I had got myself a little adapted

automatic Peugeot Cabriolet, and Sue drove me there. The car had an automatic gearbox, with a rod that ran up to the steering wheel with which one controlled the brake and petrol. It was quite tricky to get used to as one had to use a push/pull effect to either brake or give more juice. Often I would hit one or the other – and it would be the wrong one. Luckily we had no smashes.

At the testing ground this rather large, tough man in a traffic cop's uniform arrived and as he got into the passenger seat of my car, the whole car tipped to his side. He was huge, and looked like a very stern and serious man.

I thought that I would have to use every trick in the book to get him to approve my licence. So, I thought that the first thing I should do was try to arouse his sympathy and I can remember saying to him: "Did you know that I have just survived the Planet Hollywood bomb blast?" And without showing any interest, or looking at me, he said: "Ja, just drive."

And with those words I started to drive and I had to take my licence all over again. I had to stop and tail-up park, reverse, drive through tail-up bars and do all the things that beginners had to do. I was proud to get my licence first time around. Today I drive an ordinary automatic car without any problems as I can make full use of my new legs to control the brake and petrol pedals.

In another incident at that time, Carolyn took me for my weekly physiotherapy session at the Panorama Medi Clinic as I still wasn't that mobile. She suggested that instead of going directly home, we should go and have a cup of tea and something to eat in a restaurant close by.

The waitress who served us looked at Carolyn, who gave her order. No sooner had the waitress taken her order when she again looked at Carolyn, totally ignoring me in the wheelchair.

"And what will he have?" she asked Carolyn. I chipped in quickly. "My dear, it's just my legs that are damaged. There is nothing wrong with my mind." And I placed my order.

The waitress was suitably embarrassed, but it just indicated to me how people view people in wheelchairs. They think that because they are in a wheelchair, they must have some sort of mental dysfunction.

In some situations my legless state could be quite funny. I needed to buy a new pair of shoes and one day I went to Edgars to do just that. I looked at the shoes on display, found a pair I liked and asked the assistant for a pair in my size. Off she went and quickly returned with the shoes.

By this time I was sitting down and as she arrived I stood up to take the shoes from her. She held them to her defensively and said in an almost disapproving voice, "You must try them on first."

To which I replied that it would serve no purpose because I had no feet. Puzzled, she looked at my feet and said nothing; I then decided to show her my artificial legs and lifted my trousers.

The poor woman was horrified and her mouth fell open. As she dropped the box, she said: "Ag shame, sorry man".

"Don't apologise – you didn't do it," I replied. She quickly retrieved the shoes and with a new found respect assisted me all the way to the cashiers.

"If they don't fit bring them back – and I will swap them for you," was her parting shot.

In September 1999, I had some work to do in Johannesburg. It was a workshop that ended just before lunch on the last day. It was arranged that I would have lunch with friends of mine, Barry and Vivian Davies, whom I had last seen when I was still in hospital.

It was with great excitement that they fetched me from the workshop and a table had been booked at a restaurant in trendy Melville. Much catching up had to be done and of course they were delighted with the progress I had made.

Lunch was a sociable affair with much chatter and laughter as well as a few tears. A good bottle of wine was consumed. After the jovial lunch, as we were crossing the road outside the restaurant to go to the car, I heard a loud crack and suddenly felt my right leg sag.

Initially I was unaware of what had happened, and continued to walk towards the car with a heavy limp. I must have looked a sight as I limped along because Vivian suddenly got the giggles. On reaching the car, I held onto the roof and lifted my trouser leg in an attempt to see exactly what the problem was.

To my horror, my plastic leg had cracked in front of the knee. Vivian found this even funnier and her giggling got us going. We must have looked a sight: three grown people standing around the car laughing helplessly. It certainly gave new meaning to the term "legless".

Travelling in Europe in 2001, I was flying from Schipol Airport in Amsterdam to Hamburg. I arrived to check in with plenty of time and at the check-in counter, I politely asked whether I could have a window seat. The clerk told me she could not give me a boarding pass because I was on the waiting list for this flight and that I must go on standby.

I was surprised because I had booked and paid for my flights well in advance and while still in South Africa. I used the fact that I am disabled and that people were meeting me and every other excuse I could use to change the status quo, but to no avail.

Highly irritated I resigned myself for the wait. The boarding was announced and the fortunate people with boarding passes began to board. Thereafter they began calling standby passengers.

I sat and waited, growing more and more agitated. After what seemed like forever, my name was finally called. Taking my pass I went through the security checks. The metal in my artificial legs always sets all the bells and whistles in the metal detector off. Usually when I tell them of my condition, they diplomatically feel the legs and let me move on. Even in America, shortly after September 11, they allowed me to pass.

Not this time, however. A young Dutch security guard took his job very seriously and very importantly told me he wanted to do a full body search.

By this time my humour had totally run out and I was angry. We went into the cubicle and before he could tell me what to do I had let my pants fall to my plastic ankles and, sitting on the only stool in the place, dismantled my legs, removing one as well as the lining that I wear and thrust all of it into the face of the poor unsuspecting guard.

In a raised voice I asked as I thrust the leg at him, "What else do you want to see?" He was surprised and somewhat taken aback by my outburst. Seeing an angry, legless man throwing a tantrum in front of him was too much.

He fled the cubicle and I proceeded to reconnect myself. By the time I emerged from the cubicle all the passengers had boarded and they were waiting just for me. When I looked for the guard as I walked out I saw him huddled in a corner retelling his experience to his colleagues in hushed and shocked tones. I felt much better after my little outburst.

But let's get back to 1998. My uncle (my mother's brother Tommy Morgan) and his wife, Iris, came to see me when I was still recovering at home. When it was time for them to leave Tommy, very uncharacteristically, embraced me. He is normally quite a formal, reserved man, and as they were leaving that day to go home, he put his arms around me and said: "Bruce, your mother would have been so proud of you."

And indeed I think she would have been. Fortunately my mother and father were spared the trauma of my ordeal. My mother died in 1987. She had been a heavy smoker all her life, smoking something like sixty cigarettes a day and that is what ultimately got her. She died of lung cancer. A very painful and traumatic death.

My father, who had always been sickly and whom we all thought would die before my mother, outlived her and died in 1994 after an extended illness.

Unfortunately I was overseas when he died, on a six-week trip with friends. I had said goodbye to my father before leaving on my trip, but something made me phone home one day. I had a premonition to phone, and my brother told me that my father had died.

We discussed whether I should return for the funeral, but decided against it.

In hindsight, however, I wished that I had. I would have liked to have been there to say good-bye to him, despite the fact that he and I did not have the most amiable relationship when I was a child.

As the year 1998 drew to a close, I was pretty active. I spent every week seeing the physiotherapist. I worked with the occupational therapist. I was seeing my psychologist on a weekly basis. I was mobile. I was able to drive a car and I was starting to get restless. I wanted to get back to work.

In hindsight I think that I returned to work too soon. I think that ideally I should have taken some time off – perhaps a year's unpaid leave to recuperate fully before I returned to work, but I didn't.

I decided I wanted to get back to work, because I felt that our work defines who and what we are. I wanted normality and I wanted to get back to my old life.

So on the first working day of January 1999 – four months after the bomb blast – I found myself once again fighting the traffic on the N1 into Cape Town Foreshore and my office.

As I arrived in my parking space so too did my boss, Mr Ernst Ward-Cox, who came rushing over as I was battling to get out of my car.

He offered to carry my briefcase inside and it was with great delight that I was able to say: "Mr Ward-Cox, you've never offered to carry my briefcase before. I will carry it myself."

But in those months back at the office, my heart wasn't in the work. I battled. I was in great discomfort. It was awkward for me to get into the swing of things again and the position that I filled demanded a robust, energetic person and I just didn't have the energy or commitment.

It was while I was back at work in January/February that I began to see an orthopaedic surgeon about trying to get more movement in my left arm. The bones in my arm had regrown – but into a solid mass, with no elbow.

So it was that in April 1999 that I found myself, yet again, hospitalised. This time I was in the Vincent Pallotti Hospital, where I was looked after by wonderful nursing sisters and nuns of the Palatine Order.

A nun would come through on a daily basis to give me communion, which was a great comfort to me. My relationship with the nuns developed to such a degree that I was invited to attend mass in the convent where there were a lot of retired nuns.

It was very, very moving and very satisfying to sit with all these wonderful women and attend mass.

The surgeon said he would probably be able to give me a little movement around my elbow and that with a bit of luck I would be able to move my arm to about twenty-five degrees.

But the good news was that they would be able to make my arm look normal – it would not be hanging out in front of me as it had been until then.

The prognosis was that it would have minor movement, and I would be able to rest the arm at the side of my body. It would at least look normal. But, doctors warned, I would not be able to hold anything in my hand or, for instance, be able to get a fork to my mouth.

By the time the doctor came to see me (the operation had been done on the Thursday; he came to see me on the Saturday morning) I was able to place my finger right in my nose and say to him: "Look Doctor! You told me I will never be able to get a fork to my mouth. Well, I got my finger in my nose!"

Those poor physiotherapists at the Vincent Pallotti Hospital didn't know what hit them when they met me.

They inserted a tube in my arm to give me pain killers, and we forced my arm to move. Up, down, and around it would go, me sweating with pain and exertion.

I knew I wanted my arm back. I was adamant that I was going to be able to move this arm and I made them work the arm: bending it, straightening it, and bending it. From the day after the operation for weeks afterwards I used to visit them for therapy to sort out this arm.

Happily, today I have far more than twenty-five percent usage of my arm.

I had been back at work for about two months when I had to attend a business meeting at our head office in Johannesburg. I was very apprehensive about having to get on an airplane and fly to Johannesburg.

But I made plans and I found ways to get on that airplane without any assistance and to get off at the other side without any assistance; I simply climbed those airplane steps and disembarked on the other side.

The interesting thing was that when I was in the Standard Bank head office people would look at me and say: "My goodness, you look just the same." I'm not sure what they expected or how I was supposed to look, but they were quite surprised that I looked the way I did.

(Except for one person who said to me: "Gee whizz, you walk as though you have been riding a horse for the last six months!" That saying will stick with me forever.)

It was towards the end of March 1999 that I decided I couldn't continue working and that I had to resign.

I found that I spent a fair amount of my time visiting doctors, physiotherapists and psychologists. I was forever in and out of doctors' waiting rooms.

Invariably I left the office by two o'clock in the afternoon. This began to play heavily on my conscience. I didn't think it was fair to my employers; I didn't think it was fair to my colleagues and it certainly was not fair to the members of my team, for me not to be there when they needed me.

I also felt strongly that I had been spared, given a second chance at life. That I had to go out to find out why this had happened. I could not just perpetuate what I had been doing for the last 10 years after what had happened to me.

I prepared a resignation letter, thanking the bank for all they had done for me, for all their support, all their assistance and how appreciative I was. The morning I took it into my boss' office and told him what it was, he looked at me with horror.

"Bruce, we all thought that the bomb might have left you a bit brain damaged. This is proof of that."

"What do you mean by that, Mr Ward-Cox?"

"Now, more than ever you need your medical aid benefits and most certainly, you need your income."

"Mr Ward-Cox, I don't think it is fair to my colleagues, or to the bank, for me to be a passenger. I am not able to add the value that I have been able to in the past and most importantly, I want to go and find out what it is that I have been saved for," I said.

He said he would accept my resignation, but with great reluctance.

To his credit and that of Italia Bonelli and John Verster in Johannesburg, my resignation was not accepted. Instead, I was given retirement due to ill-health, which effectively ensured that I got a very small pension every month and most importantly that I still have the benefit of medical aid.

Having decided to resign, the next thing I had to do was to sell my house in Protea Valley. I had decided to join Ronald in George. My house sold quite quickly. I was hoping that I would have at least three months before I had to move but I hastily had to pack up and store my possessions. I was forced to stay in a borrowed flat belonging to some friends in Higgovale. I still had to work my notice period at the bank.

The day Stuttafords' vans pulled up to move my

stuff and we left with just a suitcase of things that I was going to take with me up to the flat, it was a very, very, very traumatic day. My heart was broken. I felt that my whole life had just fallen apart.

Having given up my job (and that by my own doing), I felt I had no real future, and now my home was gone too. All the secure, safe things that constituted my comfort zone were no longer there.

I can remember leaving the house with Tilly (who was then going to stay with her granddaughter). We locked up. We gave the key to the estate agent and we drove away. I dropped her in Milnerton, and I went on to Higgovale to the flat where I was to spend the rest of my time in Cape Town before relocating to George.

In that little flat, beneath the house in Higgovale, the tears flowed. Thank goodness – again! – for the support of Carolyn Stewart. She was there all the time.

The interesting thing is that, as Murphy's Law would have it, when the new owners moved into the house and had been there for a few weeks it became pretty obvious that they were unable to raise the finance and the whole deal fell through. So, there I was homeless, living in a flat, and serving out my notice period at the bank and having to start from scratch to resell my house.

Fortunately the house sold again quite rapidly. In June 1999 I packed the belongings I had taken with me into my little Peugeot Cabriolet and I set off to start my new life in George.

When I left the bank, I decided that I didn't want to have any major farewell functions and so just a small cocktail session was held in the bar within Standard Bank head office.

And when I left Cape Town to travel to George, I didn't want to have a major farewell either. I took a few of my very close friends, of whom Carolyn was the prime one at that stage, out for a meal and then quietly left for George, and a new life.

CHAPTER VI

CAROLYN

"In the weeks after the Planet Hollywood bomb blast I tried to deal with my own emotions. I realised that if I had gone to Planet Hollywood any earlier that evening I could have been one of the casualties – or even lost my life.

"At the same time I was supporting our injured colleagues and running the health unit at Standard Bank. This was a hard task at times as one re-evaluated life and put things into perspective.

"When people came to me to talk about their normal stress issues I often felt they were minor in comparison to what our injured colleagues were going through, having lost limbs and their loved ones.

"Most of our colleagues had support from family and friends. Bruce needed the most nursing care, hence my daily involvement in his care. I visited him in hospital – City Park where he was transferred.

"In the early days he was in the intensive care unit. It was a marvellous moment when I visited him there on the first day after he had regained consciousness, and he recognised me.

"He gradually progressed and was moved out to the general ward when he needed less nursing care. It was then that I started giving him aromatherapy massages to help ease the discomfort of his burns. The main essential oil that I used was lavender oil and the healing properties of the oil became quite apparent over a period of time.

"Not only did the oils have beneficial properties physically but on an emotional level too. Bruce found the massages to be relaxing as he listened to calming, tranquil music. It was when I could see these beneficial effects that I realised why I had studied aromatherapy.

"It wasn't long before Bruce was fitted with his new prostheses. At first he thought it would be an easy task to learn to walk on them but this wasn't the case. It took time and lots of energy as he bravely walked up and down the hospital corridor with the assistance of the physiotherapist.

"Bruce was eventually discharged from hospital and returned home to the delight of his two much loved dogs. He had a friend staying with him to manage the house and I used to call on a daily basis

117

to renew dressings on his leg, take him to the physio, doctor's appointments and support as much as possible.

"We often had long chats about how he was feeling. Some days were harder than others. I used to tell him that he was travelling a long road to recovery and he was just on a rough patch of the road.

"On the other side of this there would be a smooth patch again. I encouraged Bruce to keep a journal so that he could look back at how he was feeling on each day; he could then remind himself of the progress that he had made. He did this and it seemed to help him."

"My job at the bank continued and I took on an administrative role too for the Planet Hollywood victims. I was in regular contact with the medical aid submitting medical claims and also in touch with the Planet Hollywood Fund that had been set up to assist the victims of the bomb blast.

"Months passed and Bruce was making good progress. I was able to continue my support and encouragement for his achievements along the way.

"When Bruce was stronger, he was asked to speak at the naval college in Gordon's Bay about his experience. I remember listening to him and thinking what a real miracle man he was. He had now travelled far along the road to recovery and nothing was going to stop him along the way. He is a real survivor and has a lot of determination.

"His attitude reminded me very much of a close friend of mine, Gill Heymans, who was fighting a battle against non-Hodgkin's lymphoma. Gill was a very brave friend who always had a positive outlook on life even when her cancer returned after following a course of chemotherapy.

"Gill was using crutches as the cancer was now in her ankle bone. I introduced her to Bruce and they had an impact on each other's lives. Gill looked at Bruce thinking "What a brave guy – but at least I have my legs." Bruce looked at Gill – thinking "At least I am not battling for my life."

"Gill had a wonderful saying that she reminded herself of every day: "Every day, in every way, I am getting better." I wrote this out for Bruce so he too could benefit from this positive statement.

"Sadly Gill died a few months later but her positive attitude to life still remains with us."

"Bruce returned to work a few months later, as he was determined to get back to normality as soon as possible. By now he had learnt to drive an automatic car and become more independent. It was an emotional time for him returning to work and a period of adjustment was needed for the "new Bruce" to get used to his role again and to build up his energy levels. Throughout this time I was there for Bruce as a support and confidante.

"The Planet Hollywood blast and events have certainly had a great impact on my life. My job as occupational health practitioner at Standard Bank took on many more tasks from which I have learnt a lot. It was an emotionally draining time for me giving so much of myself to my colleagues, running the health unit and dealing with my own trauma.

"I always believe that in life you are never dealt more than you can handle, and I never questioned why I had been asked to do this.

"I learnt so much from Bruce. But the greatest thing that stands uppermost in my mind is this: that with a positive mindset, one can achieve anything in life."

CHAPTER VI

CLOSURE

I finally arrived in George in July 1999. My possessions had arrived earlier and Ronald and his friend Mimi du Plessis had very kindly unpacked them for me. So when I got there all that was left for me to do was unpack my suitcases and rearrange my personal things, like my paintings and my books, to make me feel at home.

When I purchased my house in Cape Town, my broker had advised me to take a disability waiver on my life insurance covering the bond on the house. So for a little extra every month I did. When this happened to me I was able to claim on this disability waiver and my bond was a thing of the past.

I was able therefore to put the profit from the sale of my house in Cape Town into the purchase of a new one in George. So effectively Ronald and I became 50% partners in the new home we bought.

Apart from Ronald and Mimi and her friend, Laurinda Smit, I knew nobody else in George and I was unemployed. This somehow did not faze me. I had a plan.

I had decided to find out what it was I had been spared for and the way I had decided to do this was to get involved in voluntary work – something I had never done before.

Soon after arriving in George I took myself off to the volunteers' office and announced to the startled lady that I want to get involved in some form of voluntary work.

Surprised to see a fit and healthy man making this type of offer, she did not hesitate to place a form in front of me and get me to fill it in. I listed my competencies and the type of work I could do and she said she would get back to me as soon as she could process my form.

The next day she contacted me to say that the George Child and Family Welfare was about to lose their financial adviser, and would I consider this position. I accepted without hesitation and so began a warm and rewarding relationship with child welfare.

It lasted until I finally left George to return to Cape Town. It was while I was involved with child welfare that an extraordinary thing happened.

The Catholic nuns who ran a children's home, called St Mary's, had decided it was time to hand the baton to someone else. They felt they were getting on in age, that money was tight and that crime was on the increase (one nun had been murdered recently in her room). They approached child welfare in the hope that we would take over the reigns. On doing our sums we quickly realised that we could not afford to do so on our own. At that time a group of Christians, calling themselves the "Christian Medical Services and Relief" were looking around for a building in which they could offer a one-stop medical service to the underprivileged.

We were put in touch with each other and quickly a partnership was formed. So St Mary's Children's Home, which provides shelter to 45 abused and abandoned children, was saved.

(Later a hospice for HIV/Aids women and children was opened. It is today a viable, functioning concern, providing a much-needed service to the community. I am proud to say that I was a member of the team that made this happen.)

While I busied myself with this voluntary work, work that generated an income started coming my way.

The financial services trade union, SASBO, used

me to assist their members in the Southern Cape, and Standard Bank began to involve me in ad hoc projects in George and Johannesburg.

My "inspirational" talks, in which I used my bomb experience and my subsequent journey of recovery to illustrate the point that we become the "sum of our life choices", took off.

That we either choose to journey through life as victors or victims, and that I had chosen to do so as a victor generated a lot of interest.

I was in demand to talk at church functions, schools and even corporate events. It is now five years after the bomb and there is no indication that people want to stop hearing my story.

I set up an office for myself at home and I was in business. While living in George my talks took me to New York in the November after the Twin Towers tragedy.

Sandra McDonald, a South African doctor now working in Rochester, near New York, invited me over to chat to some of her staff and patients in the aftermath of the US tragedy.

I have travelled the length and breadth of South Africa sharing my experiences.

Alison, the Port Elizabeth woman who was raped by two men, badly mutilated and left for dead in some bushes by her attackers, invited me to join her team.

Alison remains an inspiration to us all by the way she coped with her dreadful trauma a few years ago. She had set up a marketing company with her husband Tienie, to promote and market people who have inspirational stories to tell.

I was flattered by her invitation, honoured and delighted to be associated with such a person and I did not hesitate to accept her offer.

Life was good in George. I was active in the community, had met some wonderful caring, loving people and my business was doing well. Hansie Cronjé, who lived with his wife at Fancourt, was the chairman of the Disabled Sports Club in George. I met him at a function one evening, where I had been invited to be the speaker. He quietly and humbly approached the table I was sitting at after my speech. He introduced himself and complimented me on my achievements. He struck me as a gentleman, without any airs and graces.

Soon the demands of work made it clear that I would either have to move back to Cape Town or to Johannesburg. The decision was made for me in a sense when I was offered a challenging contract to work for Oncology Management Services, which is the holding group for the oncology practices with which Ronald was associated.

I accepted and in February 2003 I was on the move again, this time back to Cape Town. Today I am involved with the staff primarily at the Panorama Cancer unit, but also at the Constantiaberg unit.

I also consult for the Group's Human Resources Manager and involve myself in various in-house training and development initiatives.

I also get involved in counselling people who have lost limbs and who are not coping as a result.

My involvement with such patients began when I got a call from the Panorama Medi-Clinic. They had a young patient, only 19 years old, who had lost an arm two years ago, and now a leg, due to cancer. He was battling to cope.

Doctors, who tend to be conservative, had told him that without an arm or a leg he would find it difficult to walk. I managed to persuade him otherwise and he is mobile today.

I also continue to present my talks and consult on a wide range of human resources issues. I continue to share a house with Ronald who remains a key player in my life.

Although we no longer play squash or run in the manner we once did we still share a full life.

Ronald is an expert on "vetplante" – or lithops, and other related plants. We are always searching for new localities for various species out in the veld, and checking whether existing colonies are surviving.

I am often asked how is it that I dealt with this trauma in the constructive manner I did. Was I born emotionally strong or did I learn it in my psychology course at university? I think the answer is a little of everything.

When I was growing up I was forced, from an early age, to learn to be self-contained. If I could not do things for myself I would go without. I never depended or relied on others.

I learnt to become streetwise; today this is called having a well-developed emotional intelligence (EQ).

I was also quite vain. I did not want to go in public places in a wheelchair. I did not want people to pity me.

Further, I reasoned that I had had 45 years where I had put my legs to very good use and what the hell – I could adjust to a set of plastic ones at this stage of my life.

I was also quite naive in thinking that my adjustment would be easy. I honestly thought that it would be a piece of cake – that someone would come along and slip on these legs and off I would go.

I think if I had had the benefit of hindsight I am not sure that I would have tackled this issue with the aplomb that I did.

I always possessed a strong will. I think I was born with this trait, and could not have learnt it. I always knew what I wanted and I made plans to achieve my objectives.

I tackled this with the same determination and focus on my goals that I tackle everything else in my life.

When I decided that I would regain a full life, I very quickly realised that I had to deal with my new reality on four fundamental levels.

The first level I had to confront was the Physical. I had to come to terms with the fact that my body stopped just below my knees.

I had to learn to live with the shrapnel scars, the burn marks and the skin graft marks. I had to learn to work on what I call my plastic legs.

Initially I naively thought that someone would come along and click on these legs and I would rise up and walk. It was not to be. It was a long and painful experience. The pain was exacerbated by the fact that I developed an abscess in my right stump. The medical professionals kept telling me, when I complained about the discomfort, that it was part of the process that I had to get used to. Once my stump had taken the shape of the prosthesis, the discomfort would disappear. It never did.

The pain eventually became unbearable and it was at this stage that the doctors discovered that it was an abscess, caused by the fact that the wax used in the operation to amputate my legs had not dissolved, as it should have. As a result I was hospitalised again and the stump opened up to remove the offending object.

I had to learn to use my left arm and hand again. When the bone regrew, it did so in one solid mass. As a result I was unable to bend it at all. It simply remained at an angle of almost 90 degrees.

The nerves controlling the hand had been so severely damaged that my hand hung like a dead fish. I was unable to grasp things, let alone hold a cup or a fork. Eight months after the bomb I was again hospitalised so that some of the bone around the elbow joint could be removed.

The idea was to allow some form of flexibility in the arm. But even after the operation the doctor suggested that I should not be too optimistic about getting my hand to my mouth. A brace was designed for my hand to keep it in a certain position. As the nerves slowly repaired themselves I began to have more use of my hand. But it was my determination and that of the physiotherapists that eventually enabled me to bend my arm almost touching my shoulder with my hand and to hold objects in my hand.

Once I was able to walk on the legs unaided, after a fashion, and once I was able to use my arm and hand, I set my sights on learning to drive.

I had been driving an adapted automatic car, even with my "dead-fish" hand, but now I wanted to drive a normal automatic car without adaptations.

It is amazing how human beings adjust. I was able to sense and feel the pedals without any problem via my knees once I had my prosthesis. Today,

I drive my car like any able-bodied person would. Traffic is not an issue and on principle I do not park in allocated disabled parking bays. Parking, too, is not an issue.

My next goal in this physical domain was learning to jog again. Once in George I took myself off to the local Run/Walk for Life, run by a wonderful and patient couple, Linda and Tony Searle. I told Tony that I had no legs and that I walked on plastic ones and asked him if he thought he could teach me to jog.

Without hesitation he said he could. At the next meeting I presented myself and after doing the normal warm-up exercises with the other members, I began my walking program.

Tony decided that he would start me at the very basic level. This entailed walking slowly around a field for a period of time as a warm-up, and then a brisk walk and then again a slow walk, to cool down.

The group I walked with was a friendly bunch of people and we chatted to each other as we walked, sharing our respective war stories.

As my fitness levels increased, so too, did the distance I had to walk. I also began to alternate the walking with a jog. This was always done under Tony's watchful eye.

Eventually the day arrived when I graduated from the field to going out onto the road. That first evening was not without apprehension, but none-theless out I went, along with the group of new road users.

This I did until I felt confident enough to go at it alone. I am now able to comfortably jog five kilo-metres without any discomfort.

I have also taken part in numerous 5-kilometre fun runs and the medal I received on completion of my first one holds pride of place alongside my Comrades medal.

In the initial stages people would stare at me as I waddled past like a drunken sailor. Today, nobody gives me a second look. Very often if peo-ple don't know that I have no legs, they express surprise when they are informed. I walk quite nat-urally.

The physical level was tough, but not nearly as tough as the next level. This level was the Emotional one. On the 19th August 1998 I turned 45 years old. The bomb happened a week later on the 25th.

I had to say goodbye to the Bruce that I had known for 45 years.

The Bruce who had eventually sorted out his life. Whose career was on track, who was fit and healthy, who enjoyed the good things in life.

The Bruce who in 1994, for the first time in his life, went on an overseas trip, but who, has con-tinued to do so every year since. The Bruce, whose comfort zone was a tight, sorted-out cocoon.

And I had to confront and deal with this totally new Bruce.

This disabled Bruce, this broken Bruce. I had to be gentle with the new Bruce and build him up slowly and lovingly. If I did not love this new Bruce how could I expect anybody else to?

During this entire process I experienced the entire gamut of emotions. There were nights that I hardly slept, instead, I lay and cried. Sometimes I sobbed so hard it felt as though the sobs were coming from somewhere deep inside me.

I was angry and I got depressed and often I felt very, very sad about my loss. Little things would set me off.

I would lie in my bed and look at my shower and think that never again will I enjoy the luxury of standing having a relaxing shower. Or, I would see people running along the road and I would look longingly at their legs and my reality would hit me like a ton of bricks.

Before the bomb, whenever I found myself experiencing these negative emotions, I would put my running shoes on and the greater my depression or anger or sadness, the further I would run. After the run I would see my issues in context and in perspective. I felt better having sorted a way forward out of this negative mindset.

Clearly, I could no longer do this – especially in the beginning stages.

But I compensated, I found ways to be physical. I would wheel myself into the garden using my one good hand. I would then tip myself out of the chair with a vengeance, onto the soil and proceed to pull out of the earth anything that vaguely resembled a weed.

After a while of this frenzied activity I would feel the emotion draining away and then I would clamber back onto my chair, take myself inside, clean myself up and feel decidedly better.

As I became more mobile on my legs I was able to return to putting on my running shoes onto the plastic feet and going for a brisk walk or even a jog. And on my return I would feel much better.

Just as I knew I could not work on my body without the professional assistance of the physio and occupational therapists, I very quickly realised that I would need professional assistance in coping with all this trauma and change in my life. After chatting to a few clinical psychologists in and around Cape Town, I eventually found one I though I could relate to and work with.

She was substantially younger than I was and was a relatively newly qualified shrink. But I clicked with her and I decided she was the one I was going to use to help me to overcome this setback in my life.

And so I began to see Linda Kantor once a week. Initially she visited me in hospital and then on discharge at my home, but when I was able to walk and drive I would visit her in her rooms in the city.

She played a major role in my emotional rehabilitation.

Linda initially assisted me in dealing with the trauma of the bomb; then she helped me come to terms with my loss, and deal with my new reality.

Once we had dealt with these things, and this was not a quick fix, as my sessions with Linda went on for almost a year after the bomb, we began to unpack the emotional baggage that I had accumulated over the years.

I was confronted with issues that I had long forgotten, but which nevertheless, haunted me. We dealt with them and when the time came to terminate my therapy sessions with Linda, it was like saying goodbye to a very, very dear friend.

Today I still keep in touch with her and keep her informed of my progress. She was a key player in my journey.

The next level I had to contend with was the Intellectual. There is a wonderful Afrikaans saying, that goes, "'n boer maak 'n plan" (a farmer makes a plan). This demonstrates for me an example of winning behaviour.

When you are unsure, or do not know, you make a plan, you find a way. I did this shortly after coming home from the hospital. I did not want to use a bidet and so I found a way of getting from my bed onto my wheelchair and from there onto the toilet.

I found a way to reverse the process on completion. Not an easy task with no legs and the use of only one arm. I found a way of getting from my bed, onto the wheelchair and into the bath, without assistance.

I made plans. At no stage did I say: "It cannot be done" or "I do not know how to do it". I always said, "I will make a plan."

I was always focused on a goal. I broke any great obstacle into smaller manageable bits and set myself daily goals.

At the end on the day I would a check to see whether I had achieved my goals.

An example of this was the whole process of learning to walk on my plastic legs. I would get into my chair with my legs on my lap and wheel myself into the kitchen. I would then click on my legs and initially with great difficulty haul myself up out of the chair.

I would grasp the kitchen cupboards with everything I had and each day my goal would be to walk a distance, holding onto the cupboards for support.

Today, my goal might be to get to the first set of kitchen drawers and tomorrow a little beyond. Eventually I could get around the entire kitchen. It was painful and extremely uncomfortable and many a time I would want to give up on the idea of walking at all and remain in the chair.

But my determination, persistence and perseverance would not let me give up. From clutching the kitchen cupboards I then graduated to walking with crutches.

I had a special crutch for my left arm, called a gutter crutch. It was designed in such a manner that it accommodated my damaged unbending left arm. For my right arm I had a normal crutch.

Shortly after getting up out of the wheelchair to walk with the crutches I decided that I had to get the wheelchair out of sight and range, because the temptation to sit in it was great, especially as the discomfort and pain in my right stump developed.

I gave my chair to charity, and I am sure that it is being used by someone whose need for it is far greater then mine.

Part of this goal-focused approach was that I would not go to any public place using my crutches. The plan was that I would only go when I could walk unaided on my new legs.

With much help from the physiotherapist that day finally arrived. It happened to be a Saturday, and some friends took me to visit the local flea market.

I had warned them that they were to assist me only if I requested their help, for the rest they must let me be. I was not very stable on my new legs and balance was still an issue.

My friends were walking slightly ahead of me in an apparently unconcerned manner, with me bringing up the rear. I must have looked a sight, with my left arm stuck out at an angle in front of me while I walked in an unsteady fashion with my legs wide apart, for balance.

As I stumbled past an elderly couple, she nudged her husband and in a loud stage whisper, and a most disapproving manner said: "Look at this, nine o'clock in the morning and see how drunk he is."

My first reaction was to swing around and tell the old duck exactly what the problem was – but I thought if that was all she thought was wrong with me, there was hope that one day I would walk normally again.

The last level I had to deal with was the Spiritual. I had had a thorough Christian, Catholic grounding but in my early adulthood I had moved away from it all.

I always, however, believed in the existence of God. But at that stage in my life this belief was on my terms only. When I needed God I expected Him to be there for me, but when things were on track and going well for me, I had no need for Him.

The only time I went to church in those days was to attend weddings or funerals.

And then the bomb happened. I was initially angry with God for not allowing me to die. I prayed that I would die because I did not want to live with this broken body. I did not want to have to deal with coping with all of this and many a time I would implore Him to end it all for me.

But it was not to be. It was not His will. As I

began to deal with the reality of the bomb and as I had to confront my life and the role I had played on earth until that point, I began to realise that there was a purpose in all of this.

I made contact with a priest and began talking to God. Thanking him for the fact that I did not lose my sight in the bomb, that I am not deaf and that despite the fact I have no legs, I can still walk, drive a car and generally get around.

I began to look for the good that this dastardly deed had presented me with and when I found it I embraced it, and learnt from it. The bad I found as well, dealt with it, packaged it, discarded it and moved on.

I did not want to be a Christian in name only, however. I wanted to live my faith. When I moved to George I became a member of the local Catholic community. I got involved in a voluntary capacity with both the Cancer Association and the George Child and Family Welfare association.

This was my way of living out my Christian beliefs but also my way of thanking all the people of South Africa for their love, support, care and prayers for me when I needed them most.

My spiritual relationship grows continually and it is a wonderful feeling and a great sense of belonging to be an active part of God's family.

I am often asked by fellow Christians how I feel towards the perpetrators of the bombing. The manner in which I have dealt with them has itself been a process.

Initially, I focused all my attention and energy on achieving my goal, which was to "get my life back".

In any event they were a nameless, faceless bunch and I felt it would serve no purpose to waste time fretting about them.

But as the bombs continued in Cape Town I became very angry. Especially when Natasha Pillay, a young policewoman, lost her leg in a bomb blast on Christmas Day of the same year, and when Olivia Milner lost her leg in the St Elmo's bomb blast in Camps Bay in November 1999.

I wanted these terrorists brought to book. I wanted to see the people of Cape Town going about their business without having to think whether they would be blown away by some random bomber.

But now, five years after the bomb, I can honestly say that I have forgiven the people who did this to me.

I live with the knowledge that one day they too will have to deal with their conscience and their Creator.

I think that as we journey through life, we are constantly confronted with decisions we have to take, and choices we have to make.

It is ultimately these choices and decisions that define who and what we become. We choose to become that which we are. We become the sum of our life choices.

My experience has taught me that people choose

to fall into one of two categories. It is the quality of the choices they constantly make and the type of decisions they take that places them into one of two categories.

The first category that people choose to fall into is the group that I term the "winners" category. This type of person is self-empowering. The problems that hit them as they journey through life set them back only temporarily. After the initial shock of the unwanted change, they pick themselves up, dust themselves off and start all over again.

To fall into this category someone has to live their life according to a goal focus. They have to know what they want from life and they have to take charge, ensuring that they achieve their objective. Such people have perseverance. They achieve what they set out to achieve. They are not easily put off their goal-focused approach.

Naturally, this type of person has to have energy to do what they do throughout their lives and they almost instinctively know that they need other people to assist them in achieving their focus. Therefore, they are invariably good team players.

They are nice people to have around because they are full of go, enjoy people and get things done. As a result they are dependable and can always be relied upon to do what they undertake to do.

Like everybody else, they have setbacks and

have to deal with unwanted, intrusive change. But they manage the setback by taking charge in a persevering, goal focused manner.

As a result this type of person invariably emerges victorious from any situation, they are survivors on their life journey. They go through life triumphantly!

The second category is the category I term the "losers". This type of person chooses not to live life according to a goal focus. Instead they depend on chance, luck or good fortune.

As a result they tend to drift through life. They are constantly in and out of jobs – and relationships. They somehow lack perseverance or staying power.

They set off with great enthusiasm on projects or new tasks but quickly get bored and rapidly throw in the towel. They are unpredictable because of this lack of perseverance.

They are not always reliable or dependable people because they always seem to have a reason why they were unable to deliver, or complete a task.

When disaster hits them unexpectedly, they immediately expend most of their energy crying foul! and bemoaning the unfairness of it all. They waste the opportunity of learning from their setback and getting on with their lives in a more enriched manner.

Instead, they choose to remain rooted in one negative emotion or another. They either remain angry because this "thing" happened to them and not to someone else, or they become trapped in a depressed mode, crying and complaining to all and sundry about the unfairness of it all.

Invariably they turn to drink or drugs or both to help them deal with situations. It is almost as though they allow the unwanted tragedy or incident to control them. They become trapped by the circumstance and find it very difficult to move out of the so-called negative emotions that we all experience when some tragedy strikes us – and that some form of tragedy will intrude into your life is, I'm afraid, inevitable.

We all experience the anger, the depression and the sadness that comes with loss or drastic change. The difference between this group and the first group of people is that the first group find techniques to help them move on and out of this negative emotional cycle.

The second group however, become "victims". They blame external factors for their misfortunes and are inclined to journey through life in a "trapped" mode. They are emotionally draining, because they expend all their energy talking about "the tragedy". They become so engrossed in themselves that they do not develop an interest in others. They are not very good team players.

I think nobody would have blamed me if I had chosen to allow this intrusive tragedy to remain central to my existence.

I had every reason to blame myself.

With the spate of bombings then taking place in Cape Town, the restaurant could have done much more from a security point of view.

I could have remained bitter that this thing happened to me and not to someone else. I could have turned to alcohol to help me cope with my loss. But if I had, I would have been the loser.

I was told at various times after the bomb that the wheelchair would now be a part of my reality.

That because of the loss of my legs and the severity of the damage to my left hand and arm, I would not be able to drive a car.

That I should get someone to look after me and nurse me.

If I had not taken charge of the situation and believed in myself and actively worked towards achieving the goals I had set, I would still be sitting in that wheelchair, and I would be dependent on others to take me to wherever I needed to be.

When you lose a part of your body, you never really accept the reality of it. Not really. I still wish – and wish deeply – that I had my legs.

It is the little things that bring this back to me with some force.

Often I feel that I would love to do a simple thing like to crouch down. To feel my legs again.

To run into the sea, and feel the water around my ankles. It's such a simple thing.

When I get on board a plane, and see everyone removing their shoes and putting on the airline socks – I would really like to do that.

To deal with the loss I compensate, and rationalise. I compare myself with others who are worse off than me, and this puts my loss in perspective.

But still, a deep wish remains within me that I could be whole again.

Now when I sit down and think of my past life, where I am now and what kind of person I have become after the Planet Hollywood bomb blast, one central idea stays firmly with me.

It could be argued that before the bomb exploded in my life I was, as I put it, emotionally disabled.

I think my earlier life and hardships scarred me emotionally. I had many negative characteristics. With Linda Kantor's help I have largely addressed these issues.

I think I am now a warmer, more open, more committed person. I care much more for others. I value and cherish those who love me and in return I am not afraid to demonstrate my love for them.

Before the bomb I had a crippled soul.

I may now have a broken body – but I have a much healthier soul.

I, for one, think that is a good trade-off.

I am a better person as a result of this ordeal.

My life is rich, rewarding and satisfying. I thank God every single day for the privilege of the quality of life He has given me.

POSTSCRIPT

Where are they now

- Matty Duddy – Has retired and has recently become a grandmother. She still lives in her home in Fish Hoek. She is active and drives her own car.
- Antoinette Schoeman – Has retired and lives quietly in Kuils River, Cape Town. She shares her experience with church groups and is often invited to do so. She has no contact with Fanie's son, who has moved to Johannesburg.
- Safia Lagardien – Is a successful Human Resources/Industrial Psychologist Consultant, practising from Cape Town.
- Claire Thorndyke and Andrew Parris – Relocated

to London as planned. Today they are the proud parents of two children and Andrew is a successful accountant and Claire has advanced rapidly in the human resources arena.

- Carolyn Stewart – Went off on an overseas holiday towards the end of 1999 and met a Scotsman, Gordon Haire. They were married in 2000 and, after living in Belgium for a while, relocated recently to London, because of Gordon's work. They are the proud parents of Cameron. Carolyn's parents who lived in Durbanville now live in Scotland.

- Ronald Uijs – Has moved away from George, but remains a partner in the same oncology group. Today he works at the Helderberg Oncology Unit in Somerset West. He remains a close friend and a major player in my life.

- Garth and Shelley Walsh – Continue to live in Westville, Durban. Garth is a financial adviser. The baby with whom Shelley was heavily pregnant at the time of the bomb blast is now five. Megan Kelly Walsh and I must have had our "spirits" cross at some stage, me on the way out and she on the way in, because there exists a strong and close bond between us. Both her grandfathers are deceased and on my last visit she asked whether I would be her grandfather. Garth and Shelley have another daughter, Lauren, who was four at the time and who today remains concerned about my broken legs. Jeri Lee, Garth's eldest daughter, from a previous marriage, has recently completed matric with a very good pass. She is currently taking a "gap" year.

- Kelly Walsh – Remains in Cape Town. She is a freelance photographer and by all accounts is busy practising her craft. She was the photographer responsible for the cover of this book. We see each other on a regular basis and she keeps me informed about the remainder of the Walsh family.
- Dorothy Malan – my sister, still lives and works in the Durban area. We keep in touch on a weekly basis and I was recently in Durban to celebrate her 58th birthday.
- Gay Tyler – Has left Standard Bank and is currently employed at BP South Africa in the Human Resources department.

EMOTIONAL INTELLIGENCE

by Carl Eichstadt

Becoming a leader

Bruce's inspirational story illustrates many profound lessons about the beauty of human nature. The impact of our upbringing, of parents and key people in our lives, significant events, the strength of the human spirit, and the decisions we make shape who we become in our journey as unique human beings.

Within this milieu we have the opportunity, from time to time, to make decisions that are potentially life changing. Those people who choose to embrace these life changing decisions are what Bruce categorises as "winners".

These are people who have: insight and understanding of who they are and want to become; a desire to initiate change and view change as an opportunity; enough resolve to overcome obstacles and achieve goals; a giving nature; empathetic; confident and assertive; respected and enjoyed by others, and always prepared to learn from others.

These are the people who will demonstrate leadership in various situations.

In the modern business world, where change is constant, companies require effective leadership to achieve and sustain business success. Competitive advantage is obtained through effective leadership at all levels in a company from the person serving the customer, to the assembly of goods on the production line to the managing director and shareholders.

What is leadership?

New leadership theories and approaches focus on the transformational nature of what leaders need to do to be effective and achieve business results. Organisations tend to use the label 'manager' for roles that have the accountability and requisite authority to achieve results with and through people. It follows therefore that all managers in organizations have the opportunity to excel as a successful leader.

Leadership is about the systemic relationship: creating an inspirational vision, enabling others, nurturing trust, achieving business results and celebrating success.

- Values
- Personal excellence
- Solving complex problems
- Initiating change-innovation
- Vision
- Enabling others
- Interpersonal sensitivity
- Inspiring confidence
- Achieving results

Leadership is about achieving greatness with and through others for the benefit of all stakeholders. This could be at the level of leading an organization into a new future locally and/or globally, or leading a team to achieve more challenging productivity targets.

Effective leadership is systemic in nature requiring the continuous balance and interplay of the intellectual problem-solving and emotional intelligence-competence dimensions to achieve business results.

The pace and effectiveness by which someone acquires this competence is a function of their unique potential and intrinsic desire to lead others.

A number of theorists and practitioners suggest

that the trust, followers have in leaders is important for leadership success.

Trust is important, but a result of the demonstration of key leadership competencies.

As the trust relationship develops between the leader and followers it reinforces and further enhances the leader's competence.

Values are presumed to encapsulate the aspirations of individuals, groups, companies and societies. They relate to the most desirable, deeply ingrained standards that determine future directions and explain past actions.

Values are considered as the key in influencing the strength and direction of leadership behaviour. A value is a conception, explicit or implicit, distinctive of an individual or characteristic of a group, which influences the selection from available modes, means, and ends of action (behaviour and the results consequences of decisions and behaviour).

Important, but not exhaustive leadership values include some orientation towards people, to value people and to work with people; the desire and need to achieve; the need for a relatively independent view – opinion of the range of issues that impact on business; and integrity in all matters of business and life.

152

The leadership challenge is a journey with highs and lows which provide opportunities for continuous learning and development as a leader.

Over the past few years research has indicated that the role of emotional intelligence is critical to developing emotional competence, contributing significantly to effective leadership in organisations.

Emotional Intelligence

Think about those leaders with whom you've worked and whom you admire. It is highly likely that these people have interacted with you to the extent that you have truly felt part of the solution and its implementation. You have been inspired by these people; you may have had disagreements, but they would have been constructive; you've enjoyed your interaction with them; you will have developed yourself as a result of their coaching, you have confidence in them and will trust them to lead the business. These are people who have developed their emotional intelligence into emotional competence.

Emotional competence is "The capacity for recognising our own feelings and those of others, for motivating ourselves, for managing emotions well in ourselves and in our relationships."

Most of us can identify with feeling 'hot under the

collar', impatient, 'feeling the hair stand up on the back of your neck', feel like 'shaking or throttling' someone and many more feelings of emotional intensity. New discoveries in neurophysiology indicate that sensory signals from hearing and sight travel from the thalamus on to both the neocortex (the "thinking" brain) and the amygdala (centre of emotional intelligence) simultaneously. The amygdala is a faster processor. The amygdala's processing of information includes physiological responses (increased heartbeat, glandular secretions, etc.)

When the amygdala does not function effectively, we experience what happens when people "lose it" – they lose control and end up in a place they didn't want to be – their emotions are not used effectively; they erupt, shut down, do something extraordinarily brave, or otherwise act irrationally; on reflection they find it hard to explain why they acted as they did. Thus people feel before they think and act according to their level of emotional intelligence. Research indicates that it is possible to develop people's responses to feelings. This results in positive changes to individual and team behaviour, which improves performance. Emotional competence can be developed.

The emotional competence framework is a dynamic

interplay between self awareness, self management, social awareness and relationship management. The competence of empathy as part of social awareness leading to social skill is also a key foundation for self and relationship management. The framework is summarized as follows:

Know oneself (self awareness)

- Able to assess oneself realistically
- Has deep understanding of strengths, weaknesses, needs, and drives
- Recognises how their feelings affect them and others
- Is self-confident and candid
- Self-confidence – have a firm grasp of your capabilities

Manages feelings and impulses (self management)

- Controls bad moods and emotional impulses
- Chooses words carefully
- Avoids hasty judgments
- Steps back to consider mitigating factors and ramifications
- Creates an environment of trust and fairness

Understands social dynamics (social awareness)

- Understands how the organisation works
- Committed to helping people improve
- Senses how people are feeling
- Understands various viewpoints
- Brings conflict out into the open
- Willingly collaborates across boundaries

Advanced socially (relationship management)

- Has a knack for finding common ground with people of all kinds and has a network of people in place when the time for action comes
- Excellent at leading and working in teams
- Friendly with a purpose: moving people in the direction they desire
- Are excellent persuaders and collaborators

The past two decades have produced hard evidence drawn from many different roles, organisations and industries to demonstrate conclusively the business value of emotional competence.

The importance of emotional intelligence competencies in the role of leadership is clearly demonstrated in numerous extensive studies. The causal link between an emotional intelligence based leadership style, a healthy organisational climate and overall business performance has been conclusively established. It appears that a very significant percentage of leadership success is aligned to emotional intelligence, while at the very highest levels of leadership emotional intelligence accounts for almost the entire advantage.

The leader's style is key and four styles have emerged as relatively more effective in different situations. Leaders who have the ability to adapt to these different situations are also more effective. The four styles:

- Visionary or authoritative is most appropriate when new vision and direction are needed, to mobilise people to follow the vision, and with very strong positive impact on organisation climate;
- Affiliative style is used to motivate when the pressure is on, to heal conflicts, creating harmony, with a strong positive impact on climate;
- Democratic style is best used to build buy-in, consensus, building commitment through participation, with strong positive impact on climate;
- Coaching style is used to assist staff to improve performance and develop longer term strengths for the future, with strong positive impact on climate.

The ineffective styles of coercive and pacesetting have a negative impact on company climate.
The broader application of emotional intelligence

results in direct business benefits and includes increased staff retention, increased sales, improved decision taking, improved financial results, improved return on investment in change, faster merger/acquisition integration, increased trust and teamwork and improved productivity.

It is clear that organisations need to invest in the development of emotional competence amongst leaders at all levels. In future it will become increasingly important in sustaining organisational performance and competitive advantage.

A PSYCHOLOGICAL FRAMEWORK

by Linda Kantor

A traumatic event can be defined as one that psychologically overwhelms a person, threatening the person's integrity and capacities as a human being.

Although the word "traumatic" is often loosely used, it applies to incidents so terrifying and out of the ordinary that the individual is rendered helpless.

In the case of trauma that involves a violent act there is a greater risk of developing difficulties after the event.

The Planet Hollywood bomb blast was obviously a highly traumatic event.

Victims of trauma, in order to come out stronger on the other side, often need to rework their own story of the trauma.

Bruce's story is inspiring and encouraging to all, as he has truly been able to rework the horror of the night of the bomb blast and allow his courage and fortitude to become an inspiration to all.

It is important to understand, however, that the road towards this was one that he fought hard to achieve, and that any victim of trauma will go through some or other psychological form of working through traumatic events.

If this does not happen directly following the trauma, it can result in symptoms manifesting at some later point.

Bruce had to go through a number of psychological processes and emotions in his journey to being able to integrate the experience of having been in the bomb blast, losing his limbs, and what that meant to him.

These processes are commonly part of what Elizabeth Kubler-Ross developed in terms of the stages of loss, as follows:

DENIAL: Where the individual is unable to believe the event occurred.

ANGER: Where the individual realises the extent of his or her losses.

BARGAINING: A stage of bargaining with God or

others to reduce the effects of the trauma, or for a way out.

DEPRESSION: Where the impact of the loss sets in.

ACCEPTANCE: Reaching a stage where the person creates the ability to continue with life.

Of course the process is not a clear-cut linear one; individuals can move in and out of the various stages along the way, and some individuals never get past the denial phase.

The goal in treatment is to cope with these stages as best as one can in order to begin to live more freely.

For an individual who goes through any crisis, it is important to realise that life and the individual will be irrevocably changed. How one negotiates the stages is an important indicator as to whether one will come out the victor or the victim.

For Bruce there was at first a period of shock and disbelief.

He had to get used to the concept of the physical changes that had occurred as a result of the blast, as well as to the idea that his life had changed irrevocably.

Anger is an important and reasonable reaction to trauma, and it is important to remember that although as humans we often want to shy away from such intense feelings, a full human being does have a spectrum of emotions.

With overwhelming trauma our sense of our own efficacy is crushed, resulting in anger and frustration. Justifiably, Bruce was at times angry about the loss of his legs and the sense of powerlessness in having to learn to adjust to everyday activities, such as showering on his knees, and other severe changes in his lifestyle and capacities.

This anger can often be taken out on loved ones as it is impossible to seek out adequate revenge on those who caused the trauma itself, particularly when those responsible remain unidentified. Expression of the anger, exercise, and other more creative forms of anger management become important here.

Feeling fear is also a normal reaction to trauma. It is common for individuals to avoid the things and places that remind them of the trauma.

Such avoidance can diminish the person's quality of life and it is important that the individual does not become disabled by fear. Bruce conquered his fear by even eventually being able to go back to the Planet Hollywood venue.

It can often shatter one's perceptions that the world is a safe and reliable place, and to be able to take back one's capacity to move freely in the world is very important.

It is also common for victims of trauma to blame themselves or feel guilty for what happened. When

I first met Bruce at his hospital bed, this was his predominant emotion.

He felt that he had somehow been responsible for his staff and for what happened. These feelings are often related to the sense of powerlessness that individuals are left with; where they feel that some action on their part could have prevented the experience.

By blaming themselves they attempt to find a feeling of control.

Sadness and grief are also a critical part of recovery.

For example, Bruce had the wisdom at some point to just allow himself three days of grief, where he simply felt the sadness about his life change and truly questioned why his life had been spared and whether he wanted to continue with it.

He was also able during that process to make a decision not to just remain caught up in grief. Grieving is an important emotion on the road to healing.

Often in western society excessive grief is considered a weakness or a sign of self-pity. This attitude can be harmful to those who have experienced the trauma and then feel abandoned and left to deal with it.

It is of course important to learn how to share one's grief and feelings of vulnerability and fragility, and to see the capacity to do so as a sign of psychological strength, rather than weakness.

One must be allowed time to grieve for the loss, to examine that loss, and then to put it into perspective – and plan a future despite all you have lost.

It is important to note the importance of time in dealing with grief, and it can be beneficial to take time out from work if the grief is unmanageable.

A number of factors will assist an individual in reducing his or her chances of developing a more ongoing post-traumatic stress syndrome.

Firstly it is important that the individual has the support of others. Often just knowing that there is someone out there who cares enough can lessen the trauma. The role of Ronald and Bruce's brother Garth were therefore crucial and I believe that Bruce was aware of their love and support right from the start. (It is of course more difficult for individuals who suffer a more shameful trauma such as rape).

Having access to a safe and secure environment also allows one the freedom to heal, and the home Bruce lived in was certainly that. Of course financial assistance and care are also crucial, and the response of his company certainly was the correct one in terms of assisting him in his healing.

Bruce was aware from the start of the importance of his psychological well-being. He explored a variety of options before he chose his therapy treatment with me. Despite my relative inexperience I believe he chose a therapist he felt he could relate to, and with whom he felt safe enough to share his difficult journey.

His therapy became a place where he could freely explore and express his emotions about the bombing and also about his life prior to the bombing. I also believe however that there was much in Bruce's favour in terms of his attitude to help him make the psychological transitions necessary to turn a horrific experience into an essentially positive one.

Mastery can be seen to include some important factors.

Firstly, it is the ability to take control of difficult situations. The psychological concept of locus of control is important here.

Individuals with a more internal locus of control, who take responsibility for the events and problems in their lives, are obviously better able to recover.

In contrast, those who more often blame external events for their circumstances in life will struggle more to recover. (This does not diminish the importance of the anger phase, where the individual is rightly angry about the trauma and its effects.)

Because of his internal locus of control, Bruce was able to commit to taking good care of himself through exercise and the therapies that he felt would help him to recover.

Those who master a trauma more effectively often gather and identify the information and the help that they need. They are able to look at all possibilities or, in Bruce's case, treatment options, and then have the will to follow through on treatment plans and goals.

They are also able to access the effectiveness of what they are choosing to do, and then to attempt something different if necessary.

Mastery is also about their being able to make peace with circumstances that cannot be changed and, particularly in Bruce's case, they are often able to make a contribution, and a difference with what they have learnt from their trauma.

In addition to the support of friends and family, Bruce became committed to projects and causes that he believed in. It is important to be able to have this kind of outlet, and more so to develop and deepen one's sense of meaning in life. (Acts such as the bomb blast can leave individuals apathetic and devoid of understanding and meaning in their lives.)

Such coping skills are for the most part learnt as we grow up; either from role models around us, or from learning about what works when we are faced with difficulties. Bruce's experience with the bullies in his early school years was clearly a strong training ground. He is a clear example of how even if there are no strong support structures or role models at home; such skills can be learnt along the way.

Bruce discusses in his story the role of the spiritual on his journey to healing. For some individuals trauma can pose serious questions in terms of one's faith and belief systems. For Bruce, the bomb blast signalled a move back towards his religion of origin, and this allowed him to deepen his relationship with God. Once again it is important to note that this too is a process which can have many twists and turns along the way.

Finally it is important to mention that often when there is trauma, it is not only the person present in the event that will experience trauma, but those close to the individual can experience secondary trauma. If that is the case it is important that support be offered to relatives and partners, so that they can offer the trauma victim the best possible help.

It is important to note that it inevitably takes time to work through the impact of traumatic events. One cannot predict the time it might take for an individual to accept the implications of the event. About 30% of individuals who go through a trauma develop some psychiatric symptoms.

In some cases the symptoms may remain severe, or persist for so long that they affect normal functioning. This is known as post-traumatic stress disorder (PTSD). Individuals with PTSD experience intrusive thoughts and feelings about the trauma, resulting in feelings of helplessness, or psychic numbing. It is even more important in these cases to receive psychological help early on.

The impact of any trauma really depends on the meaning of the situation for the person, as it is not the stressor (that which caused the trauma) but the way the individual reacts to the stressor that is important.

This is why talk therapy can be very beneficial as putting painful feelings into words reduces the internal pressure of the emotions.

Sybrand Mostert is an award-winning journalist and editor who has worked for the major newspaper titles in South Africa during his 20-year career. He is now a freelance writer living in Cape Town and contributes to a variety of local and international publications.